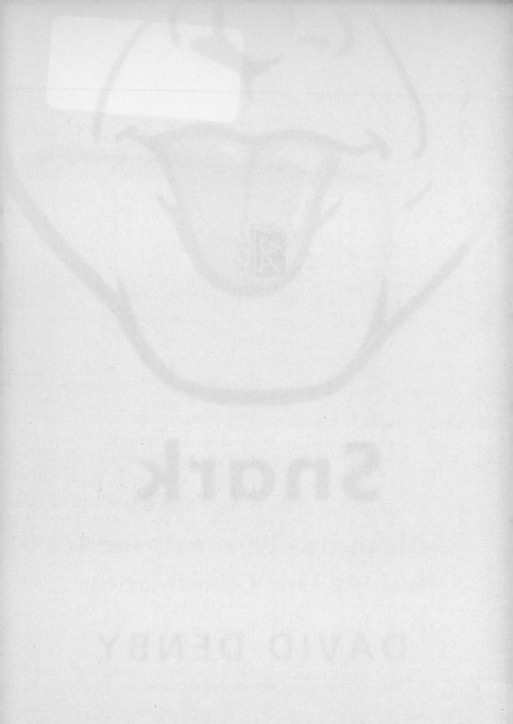

ALSO BY DAVID DENBY

———

American Sucker
Great Books

Snark

A POLEMIC IN SEVEN FITS

---◆---

David Denby

Simon & Schuster Paperbacks

NEW YORK LONDON TORONTO SYDNEY

Simon & Schuster Paperbacks
A Division of Simon & Schuster, Inc.
1230 Avenue of the Americas
New York, NY 10020

First Simon & Schuster trade paperback edition January 2010

SIMON & SCHUSTER PAPERBACKS and colophon are registered
trademarks of Simon & Schuster, Inc.

For information about special discounts for bulk purchases,
please contact Simon & Schuster Special Sales at
1-866-506-1949 or business@simonandschuster.com.

The Simon & Schuster Speakers Bureau can bring authors to
your live event. For more information or to book an event,
contact the Simon & Schuster Speakers Bureau at
1-866-248-3049 or visit our website at www.simonspeakers.com.

Designed by Paul Dippolito

Manufactured in the United States of America

10 9 8 7 6 5 4 3 2

The Library of Congress has cataloged the hardcover edition as follows:
Denby, David.
Snark : a polemic in seven fits / David Denby.
p. cm.
1. Invective. 2. Invective—Humor. 3. Wit and humor—Social aspects. I. Title.
PN6231.I65D46 2009
809'7—dc22   2008050435

ISBN 978-1-4165-9945-6
ISBN 978-1-4165-9946-3 (pbk)
ISBN 978-1-4391-1008-9 (ebook)

For Susan Rieger

For the Snark *was* a Boojum, you see.

—Lewis Carroll, "The Hunting of the Snark"

The hunt for snark never ends.

—Clive James, literary critic

Author's Note

Lewis Carroll's extraordinary and menacing nonsense poem, "The Hunting of the Snark," published in 1876, was subtitled "An Agony, in Eight Fits." It seems that *fit* was still extant in Victorian England as a term for "canto." I have had one fewer fit than Lewis Carroll, yet I have retained his word. But more of this in the Second Fit.

Contents

Snark

The Republic of Snark

———·•·———

In which the author lays out the terrain of his momentous
subject, defines the nature of snark, and distinguishes among
high, medium, and low versions of the unfortunate practice.

T his is an essay about a strain of nasty, knowing abuse spreading like pinkeye through the national conversation— a tone of snarking insult provoked and encouraged by the new hybrid world of print, television, radio, and the Internet. It's an essay about style and also, I suppose, grace. Anyone who speaks of *grace*—so spiritual a word—in connection with our raucous culture risks sounding like a genteel idiot, so I had better say right away that I'm all in favor of nasty comedy, incessant profanity, trash talk, any kind of satire, and certain kinds of invective. It's the bad kind of invective—low, teasing, snide, condescending, knowing; in brief, snark—that I hate.

Perhaps a few contrasts will make the difference clear. Jon Stewart and Stephen Colbert can be rough. Like all entertainers, they trust laughs more than anything else, and they wait for some public person to slip a stirrup and fall. "We're carrion birds," says

Stewart, a man capable of describing Karl Rove as having a head like a lump of unbaked bread dough. But the Stewart/Colbert claws are sharpened in a special way. Even when pecking at a victim's tender spots, they also manage to defend civic virtue four times a week. When Stephen Colbert, a liberal, wraps himself in the flag and bullies his guests in the manner of right-wing TV host Bill O'Reilly, he is practicing irony, the most powerful of all satiric weapons. Attacking the Bush administration, Colbert and Stewart were always trying to say, *This is not the way a national government should behave.* Snark, by contrast, has zero interest in civic virtue or anything else except the power to ridicule. When the comic Penn Jillette said on MSNBC in May 2008, that "Obama did great in February, and that's because that was Black History Month. And now Hillary's doing much better 'cause it's White Bitch Month, right?" he was not, putting it mildly, practicing irony or satire. The remark was bonehead insult, but insult of a special sort. It spoke to a knowing audience—to white people irritated by black history as a celebration, and to men who assume an ambitious woman can safely be called a bitch. The layer of knowingness, in this case, was an appeal to cranky ill will and prejudice. Jillette's joke was snark. A question I found as a comment on a right-wing blog—"Is Obama a fat-lipped nigger—or what?"—is simple racist junk. But a student named Adam La-Duca, formerly president of the Pennsylvania Federation of College Republicans, wrote on his Facebook page that Obama was "nothing more than a dumbass with a pair of lips so large he could float half of Cuba to the shores of Miami (and probably would)." That remark, in its excruciating "humor" and its layer of knowing reference, is tin-plated snark (and also racist junk).

Snark is not the same as hate speech, which is abuse directed at groups. Hate speech slashes and burns, and hopes to incite, but without much attempt at humor. Some legal scholars—most notably, Jeremy Waldron, of New York University—have argued that the United States, a tumultuous, multiethnic country with many vulnerable minorities, should consider banning hate speech by law, as some countries in Europe have done. But that is not my concern here; the legal issues lie far beyond the range of this essay, and, in any case, I am against censorship in any form, on the usual ground that it will choke legitimate critical speech as well as vicious rant. I will hunt the snark but leave hate speech alone. I will also ignore the legions of anguished, lost people on Web sites and the social networking site Facebook who are convinced that, say, Barack Obama is the Antichrist ("Buraq was the name of Muhammad's horse!"), and who fly about wildly, like bats trapped in a country living room, looking for a way to release fear. Madness and paranoia are not the same as snark.

Nor am I talking about the elaborately sadistic young sports known on the Internet as "trolls." These are technically enabled young men, part hackers, part stalkers, who pull such pranks as teasing the parents of a child who has committed suicide or sending flashing lights onto a Web site for epileptics. The lights may cause seizures. Fun! The trolls have a merry time screwing people up. What they do violates existing statutes,* and if federal and state authorities had the energy and resources to pursue them, the trolls could probably be prosecuted for harassment. So far they have gone largely unpunished, but I leave them to the cops and prosecutors. Finally, I will bypass the issue of political correctness, which, rightly or wrongly, is a way of protecting groups against calumny and lesser slights. Political correctness actually

---

* See Mattathias Schwartz's report in the *New York Times* of August 3, 2008, for the details.

shares one leading characteristic with snark—it refuses true political *engagement,* the job of getting at the truth of things. All too often, PC tries to rein in humor that might brush against a truth. What I'm doing here—hunting the snark—is a way of preserving humor. Those of us who are against snark want to humble the lame, the snide, and the lazy—and promote the true wits.

Snark attacks individuals, not groups, though it may appeal to a group mentality, depositing a little bit more toxin into already poisoned waters. Snark is a teasing, rug-pulling form of insult that attempts to steal someone's mojo, erase her cool, annihilate her effectiveness, and it appeals to a knowing audience that shares the contempt of the snarker and therefore understands whatever references he makes. It's all jeer and josh, a form of bullying that, except at its highest levels, beggars the soul of humor. In the 2000 presidential campaign, Maureen Dowd of the *New York Times* had Al Gore "so feminized and diversified and ecologically correct, he's practically lactating" in one column and buffing his pecs and ridging his abs in another column. Which was it? Effeminate or macho? Snark will get you any way it can, fore and aft, and to hell with consistency. In a media society, snark is an easy way of seeming smart. When Harvard professor Samantha Power resigned from Obama's campaign on March 7, 2008, after calling Hillary Clinton "a monster," Michael Goldfarb's comment, on the blog of the conservative magazine the *Weekly Standard,* was "Tell us something we don't know." Power's remark is a plain insult; Goldfarb's, with its cozy "we," which adds a twist of in-group knowingness, is snark. Snark doesn't create a new image, a new idea. It's parasitic, referential, insinuating.

Of course, snark is just *words,* and if you look at it one piece at a time, it seems of piddling importance. But it's annoying as hell, the most dreadful style going, and ultimately debilitating. A future America in which too many people sound mean and silly, like small yapping dogs tied to a post; in which we insult one another merrily in a kind of endless zany brouhaha; in which the lowest, most insinuating and insulting side threatens to win national political campaigns—this America will leave everyone, including the snarkers, in a foul mood once the laughs die out. At the moment, there are snarky vice presidential campaigns (Sarah Palin's mean-girl assault on Barack Obama as "someone who sees America as imperfect enough to pal around with terrorists who targeted their own country . . . This is not a man who sees America like you and I see America."); snark-influenced crafts (advertising); an enormous, commercially flourishing snark industry (celebrity culture); snarky news-and-commentary cable TV shows, left and right; and snark words, such as *whiny* and *whiner,* which are often used to cut the ground under anyone with a legitimate complaint. Senator John McCain, displaying some creative flair in his attacks on Barack Obama on October 15, 2008, added a snarky visual effect (perhaps a first in a presidential debate) to ordinary sarcasm, by holding up his fingers for air quotes around the word *health* in a discussion on abortion: "Here again is the eloquence of Senator Obama—the 'health' of the mother. You know, that's been stretched by the pro-abortion movement in America to mean almost anything." By using air quotes (was he channeling the late Chris Farley?), McCain was sending a sportive signal to pro-lifers—that's the snarky part—but also suggesting, perhaps unconsciously, that the heath of the mother was somehow irrelevant to the matter of abortion. At the end of the first decade of the twenty-first century, snark sounds like the seethe and snarl of an unhappy and ferociously divided country, a country

releasing its resentment in rancid jokes. It's a verbal bridge to nowhere. I've been accused of writing some myself.*

The practice has often been mislabeled. Snark is not the same
thing, for instance, as irreverence or spoof. I've heard the morally
outraged satirist Lenny Bruce described as a pioneer of snark,
which is absurd. Bruce, in his way, was as serious as the prophet
Jeremiah. David Letterman the ironist is snarky; Jay Leno, a
straight joke teller, is not. Don Rickles takes on hecklers and insults his audience, but his act is a formal structure whose unvary-
ing rules are known in advance. If he weren't vicious, people
wouldn't go to hear him. What he does isn't snark; it's a harmless, self-contained ritual performed by a cobra with a ribbon tied
around its head.

The platonic ideal of snark is something like this: Two girls are
sitting in a high school cafeteria putting down a third, who's sitting
on the other side of the room. What's peculiar about this event is
that the girl on the other side of the room *is their best friend.* In that

---

* The actor Owen Wilson, holding forth to Page Six of the New York Post,
threatened to punch me out once when I wrote, in the New Yorker, an attack on
the work of his friend Ben Stiller. At the time (January 2005), Stiller was wildly
overexposed in movies. This may be the passage Wilson objected to: "[Stiller's]
face seems constructed by someone playing with the separate eyes, noses, and
mouths of a children's mix-and-match book. There's nothing wrong with the
features, but they don't quite go together. His forehead is high; his eyes sink into
caves; his long jaw breaks into a surprisingly wide, sometimes friendly, sometimes scary, grin. Stiller knows how to use his big head for broadly obvious
comic effect: if he pulls down his chin and stares, he looks like a mildly paranoid
gibbon, and by furrowing his brow and twisting his mouth, he can do a dozen
variations on dopey suspiciousness, manic glee, or pawing-the-dirt sexual rage."
Reading it over, I thought the physical description was juicy—okay, nasty. But
is it snark? I leave it to the reader to decide.

scenario, snark is abusive or sarcastic speech that operates like poisoned arrows within a closed space. Its intention is to offer solidarity between two or more parties and to exclude someone from the same group. On *Gossip Girl,* this is juicily entertaining, but in real life it's as hostile as spit. The crab that tries to escape the barrel—the girl who dresses differently or studies harder—gets pulled back into the barrel. Who does she think she is? A young writer who creates an ambitious work of fiction gets snarked by journalists of lesser ambition. What a pretentious phony! Snark often functions as an enforcer of mediocrity and conformity. In its cozy knowingness, snark flatters you by assuming that you get the contemptuous joke. You've been admitted, or readmitted, to a club, though it may be the club of the second-rate.

Let's not fall into a misunderstanding. Life would be intolerable without any snark at all. There are public events like Dick Cheney's shooting his close friend in the puss, or Eliot Spitzer's encounters with a $4,300 hooker after prosecuting vice for several years—events that no human being could fail to relish, rehash, retell. These misadventures inspired snarky comments by the hundreds, and all one can say about the comments is that malice is as natural as kindness, and that someone completely without snarky impulses would have little humor of any sort. One can't, without hypocrisy, be against all snark all the time. The practice exists at different levels of ambition and skill, and at the top levels snark crosses into wit. In a 1976 essay ("Some Memories of the Glorious Bird and an Earlier Self"), Gore Vidal, a master of high snark, recounts the early days of his friendship with Tennessee Williams. Eventually, the narrative turns to Truman Capote:

> *Capote would keep us entranced with mischievous fantasies about the great. Apparently, the very sight of him was enough*

to cause lifelong heterosexual men to tumble out of unsus-pected closets. When Capote refused to surrender his virtue to the drunken Errol Flynn, "Errol threw all my suitcases out of the window of the Beverly Wilshire Hotel!" I should note here that the young Capote was no less attractive in his person then than he is today.

This is funny no matter how you read it. But the last line achieves its full snarky glory only if you know that in 1976, when Vidal wrote these sentences, Capote was a sodden mess. Vidal's insult is perfectly phrased. How could one be against it? A writer like the Roman poet Juvenal (discussed in the Second Fit), who deploys a virulent, sometimes obscene wit—an early case of snark, I think—can make proper writers seem timid and slow.

Another, more complicated example of contemporary high snark—or, rather, attempted high snark: The literary editor and critic Leon Wieseltier reviewed *The Second Plane,* a collection of essays about Islamic extremism by the English writer Martin Amis, in the *New York Times* of April 27, 2008, and, at great length, Wieseltier deplored Amis's lack of seriousness. Amis, he wrote, used the catastrophe of 9/11 to show off his brilliant phrasemaking; instead, he should have tried—more soberly and with better information—to understand the nature of radical Islam. Wieseltier's clinching judgment goes like this: "Pity the writer who wants to be Bellow but is only Mailer." Now, this is a knowing signal to readers who believe that Saul Bellow was a greater writer than Norman Mailer. Yet it's an odd insult, since most of us would hardly turn scarlet with shame if Mailer's *The Armies of the Night* or *The Executioner's Song* suddenly turned up on our résumé. What is there to "pity"? In that respect, Wieseltier's remark is a misfire. In another respect, it's a stealth dart aimed directly at Martin Amis's heart. An even smaller group of readers would know that Amis adores Bellow's work and dislikes Mailer's. The snark is unspoken: *You write like someone you despise, not like your hero.*

At the more popular level, there is a fine piece of wickedness perfected by the British humor magazine *Private Eye.* In the sixties, a British woman journalist, disappearing from a London party, had a pleasing encounter with a former cabinet minister in the government of Ugandan dictator Milton Obote; afterward, reappearing, she said that the two were "upstairs discussing Uganda." Thereafter, and for decades, whenever any public figure was taunted by the magazine for illicit sex, he or she was described as having "Ugandan discussions." The British libel laws are tougher than ours; the Uganda euphemism (and there were others) began as a way of avoiding libel, but it became a snazzy repeated joke, an insult that gathered laughter around it every time it was applied to a new victim. The two hundred thousand or so readers of *Private Eye* gloried in a gag that united them within the walls of an exclusively knowing club. "Ugandan discussions," a terrific piece of mid-snark, is much funnier than anything appearing in America today.

At what point do we write snark out of the book of life—or at least out of the book of style? When it lacks imagination, freshness, fantasy, verbal invention and adroitness—all the elements of wit. When it's just mean, low, ragging insult with a little curlicue of knowingness. Much of what passes for humor in American public discourse strikes me this way, and, in the Fourth Fit, I will set out the way snark is written today—a kind of stylebook of snark—and give examples. If you crave immediate proof, turn to the discussion threads that follow a routine post on so many Web sites. For every bright and easy conversation, there's another one that turns into a free-fire zone of bilious, snarling, resentful, other-annihilating rage, complete with such savories as racist taunt, nationalist war whoops ("Fuck those towel-heads"), misogynist rant, gay-baiting witticisms. In these effusions, snark is the preferred mode of attack. Everyone, it seems, wants to be a comic. I would bet that half the words written as instant messages or Twitter are snark of one sort or another. As for commenters, they don't just address the famous and powerful; they light into one another. You can't miss them if you look, and even a man as generous as Walt Whitman would be hard-pressed to hear in these flares the barbaric yawp of a free people. Then there are the college men writing on such sites as Juicy Campus who have slept with a woman and then refer to her as "a whore" by name while hiding behind anonymity (snark is their preferred mode of attack, too; more on this in the Fifth Fit). Low snark, in its current variety, is a degeneration of invective into smear or just dull slagging, and it shows up in professional venues, too—in gossipy celebrity and sports sites; in daily and weekly newspapers desperately trying to reach young readers and hoping that a snippy-snappy tone is the way to do it.

It turns out that in the wake of the Internet revolution, snark as a style has outgrown its original limited function. The Internet has allowed it to metastasize as a pop writing form: A snarky insult, embedded in a story or a post, quickly gets traffic; it gets linked to other blogs; and soon it has spread like a sneezy cold through the vast kindergarten of the Web. Not only that, it's there forever, since it's easily Googled out of obscurity. Along with all the useful, solid, clever, playful information and opinion circulating around, a style of creepy nastiness is rampaging all over the place, too. The zombies are biting, and a hell of a lot of us are enjoying the spectacle. The Internet did not invent sarcasm, or the porous back fence where our gossiping parents gathered, or the tenderly merciful tabloids; but it provides universal distribution of what had earlier reached a limited number of eyes and ears. In brief, the knowing group has been enlarged to an enormous audience that enjoys cruelty as a blood sport.

No one should take this essay as a request that all the angry people curl up in someone's lap and purr. Savage insult, especially insult directed at the powerful, is a necessary part of democratic culture, and in some ways we live in a great age of comedy and popular satire. Talent jumps up out of nowhere on some of the blogs, joining up with people like Sacha Baron Cohen, Chris Rock, Tina Fey, and Sarah Silverman; Jon Stewart and Stephen Colbert; the crew at *Saturday Night Live;* the people who put out the satirical rag *The Onion;* the creators of *The Simpsons* and *South Park* and *Family Guy.* These are culture heroes, and rightly so, and they don't practice snark but something finer, or something crude and free, bold and happy—satire, spoof, lampoon, burlesque, all heaven-sent forms. They are entertainers, but sometimes much more. I will take a quick, admiring look at some of their forebears—the origins of snark in the noisy drinking clubs of ancient Greece; the poets and orators who practiced invective as a formal mode in classical Athens and Rome; the devastating eighteenth-century conservative wits Pope and Swift; the Oxford cutups and cutthroats who started *Private Eye* in the sixties; the media-savvy men who penetrated the walls of the famous in *Spy* magazine, the premier outlet for American snark in the eighties. In contemporary writing, snark has entered a degenerate phase, and I will try to distinguish between harshly funny satirical writing and trivial kneecapping.

Parts of my argument are directed at a medium in which professional and nonprofessional writers mix together freely, exuberantly. Why argue for decency, civility, style, *grace* in the Internet? In a medium which, by its very nature, is free to all comers, talented and untalented, cheerful and enraged, pure and impure alike? Why would anyone set up a tearoom with linens and silver in the middle of the saloons of the Wild West? What's at stake? Well, the frontier is now absorbing the traditional elite settlements of journalism: The network news broadcasts and many newspapers and magazines are slowly, hesitatingly, but inevitably sliding into the Internet, sometimes using online sites as an adjunct, sometimes as a principal venue. This massive, sliding-cargo movement leaves established editors and writers worried, and not just because they fear unemployment. In the near future, the authority of agreed-upon facts and a central narrative of what's going on in the world could weaken and even dissolve. The Internet is remarkably adept at amplifying, correcting, ridiculing, and overturning that narrative, but it cannot, on its own, create it. In the Internet, there will be no such authority, only the many niches and bat caves from which highly colored points of view will fly wildly like confused vectors, and in that situation, no one will be right, no one will be wrong, and everything will be a matter of opinion. In that future dystopia, the most memorable bits of invective and sarcasm will attain the widest currency, and snark will reign supreme.

We are in a shaky moment, a moment of transition, and I think it's reasonable to ask: What are we doing to ourselves? What kind of journalistic culture do we want? What kind of Internet culture? What kind of national conversation? My "position" regarding the Internet is this: *We have this incredible tool. Let's not screw it up.* As for the mainstream press, those of us not too blinkered and panicked to notice the dreadful writing that passes itself off as fun (both in the Internet and our own work) will want to stop the spread of that stuff. Journalism is a vast sea of good and bad, but surely some demands can be made, and the distinction between toughness and cynicism, incisiveness and fatuous sarcasm, satire and free-floating cruelty—these are differences worth fighting for in any medium. There's no need to sober up. But we can certainly toughen up.

A Brief, Highly Intermittent History of Snark, Part 1

*In which the author celebrates the fantastic and
sinister origins of the word and then describes the way
the habit has fared in the hands of selected authors,
both ancient and modern.*

Genealogy of a Word

In 1874, the Reverend Charles Lutwidge Dodgson was visiting his sister in the town of Guildford, England, when he was struck by a most peculiar lightning bolt. A real zigzag. As he later recalled (or reconstructed) the event, he was strolling on a hillside when suddenly a single line of verse came into his head: "For the Snark *was* a Boojum, you see." The *what* was a *what*? Dodgson's pen name, of course, was Lewis Carroll; he was the author of *Alice in Wonderland* (1865) and its sequel, *Through the Looking-Glass* (1871), two classic children's books which teased nonsense into wounding sense. Carroll had his mysteries, light and dark. Some years after his stroll, he wrote of the inspiration on the hillside, "I knew not what it meant, then; I know not what it means, now." As for the word *snark*, he later told a friend it was also pointless—nothing more than a combination of snail and shark. Nevertheless, the rest of a long poem "pieced itself together," as he put it, over the next two years. "The Hunting of the Snark: An Agony, in Eight Fits" was published for Easter, in 1876. This mock epic is perhaps the greatest example of nonsense verse in the English language.

"The Hunting of the Snark" chronicles a voyage and an adventure. Representatives of Victorian society—a baker, a banker, a barrister, a broker, a billiard-marker, a shoe-polishing servant known as Boots—joined by a beaver, and led by the captain, or Bellman, board a ship, travel to the ends of the earth, and search for a mythical beast that they must kill, the snark. What *is* this beast? The snark has some specific attributes (among other things, it has no sense of humor and can't stand puns), but what, exactly, the snark looks like, and why the men so badly want to kill it, Carroll never tells us. At least, not in any intelligible form. The entire poem, dancing into dead ends or tiptoeing politely into brilliant irrelevancies, builds up to the line that came to Carroll on the hillside, and that line, when it arrives, is a moment of terror.

We were partially set up for it earlier. In Fit the Third, one of the crew, the anxious baker, tells the rest of the party something he had once heard from his uncle. The snarks are harmless, the uncle had said—harmless, except for one variety of snark:

> But oh, beamish nephew, beware of the day,
> If your snark be a Boojum! For then
> You will softly and suddenly vanish away,
> And never be met with again!

But despite this warning, the baker is annihilated. He ventures off the ship, encounters a snark, cries "It's a Boo—," and disappears in midsentence. He just vanishes into nowhere. And then Carroll repeats his inspiration on the hillside: "For the snark *was* a Boojum, you see." And that is the end of the hunt, the end of the poem. Afterward, recovering from shock, we may begin to wonder: Since the men don't find any other snarks, perhaps there aren't any—that is, not any of the harmless variety. Perhaps *all* snarks are Boojums. Either you kill them, or they kill you.

The beast that can be named but not quite described, terrors that have to be slain or they make you disappear—these might not be considered among the likely fears of a man who was in all outward respects a great success. Wealthy from his literary work, and socially well connected, Lewis Carroll, in 1876, was known as a rather prim forty-two-year-old bachelor, a lecturer in mathematics at Christ Church College, Oxford, and the author of two enormously popular and distinguished books. The Victorians did not necessarily see anything odd, as we do, about his intense repeated friendships with eight- and nine-year-old girls. For years, Carroll, as a young man, had been close to the Liddells, a family in Oxford that included three little girls, including the child who may have been the original of Alice. But, in 1863, something went wrong. An undisclosed scandal caused his removal from the family. Who knows what obsessions and fears Carroll carried around with him? "The Hunting of the Snark" is very funny—people who memorized it as children can reel off long passages at will—but a cloud of menace hangs over the entire poem. Carroll sometimes goes past play into real perversity, and the ending is a stunner. As Carroll used it, there was something sinister, hidden, and destructive in the nonsense word from the beginning. The snark is the thing that makes you disappear.

Carroll says he made the words up, but, according to the *Oxford English Dictionary, snark* was hanging around in other languages, so Carroll may have heard it somewhere or other. In Swedish and Norwegian, *snarka,* and, in German, *snarken,* echoed the sound of snoring or snorting. I can't do much with snark's derivation in snoring. In its imitation of a *snort,* however, snark unveils its later habit of contemptuous dismissal. Intimations of snarly ill-temper cling to the word's foreign versions. And Carroll's fantastic use of it has a potent echo. From time to time, some of the people who professionally attack others have boasted that their words are strong enough to make their victims disappear— go away, give up, even kill themselves. *Their* snark is definitely a Boojum—at least, as they tell it. But more on that in a minute.

As the word passed through Carroll and attained currency in English usage, it gave up its life as both a snort and a mythical beast, and it picked up a new meaning. If you nagged at someone, you were snarking him. In her 1904 tale *The Phoenix and the Carpet,* another wonderful children's book writer, E. Nesbit, wrote the following sentence: ". . . he remembered how Anthea had refrained from snarking him about tearing the carpet." That's closer to the modern meaning of finding fault. In the years after Nesbit, the word, as far as I can tell, was used only occasionally, but it reemerged in the sixties. The Irish poet Paul Muldoon tells me that, growing up in Belfast in the sixties, he heard *snarky* used as we use it now. If you were snarky, you were teasing someone, trying to get at him. Also in the sixties, Richard Crossman, the writer and Labor MP, and later minister of housing and local government in Harold Wilson's cabinet, noted in his diary that "[w]e also have to overcome something else—the stream of anti-government propaganda, smearing, snarky, derisive, which comes out of Fleet Street."

So there, in Crossman's diary, you definitely have the word in its current meaning, though others, before and after the sixties, have made use of *snark* in their own way, perhaps because they merely liked the ugly, blunt sound of it, the single harsh syllable that expels a puff of insolent air in its wake. The writer and adventurer Jack London, who loved small boats and who enjoyed an exciting sexual relationship with his second wife, Charmian, had a two-masted ketch built according to his own design, the *Snark*, in which he hoped to spend seven years with Charmian sailing around the world. The voyage lasted two years, from 1907 to 1909, ending when London became ill. In the book that he wrote in 1911, *The Cruise of the Snark*, he said, "We named her the *Snark* because we could not think of any other name—this information is given for the benefit of those who otherwise might think there is something occult in the name." This leads nowhere in particular (the *Snark* was a beautiful but leaky craft), yet the name stuck: Even now snarks are a kind of light sailboat. A Corporal Snark—sneaky and unpleasant—turns up in Joseph Heller's *Catch-22*, which was published in 1961. There are video-game characters called snarks, and the United States has an intercontinental nuclear cruise missile called the SM-62 Snark, which, I understand, can be insulting in a fairly insistent manner.

Primal

The word's meaning, and its transformations and variations before it reaches its modern power, is merely a fascinating curiosity. What of the act itself? The hunt for the snark never ends; it goes way, way back. Obviously, there have always been mockers, some talented, some merely crass, but let us seek the unholy birth of the act as we understand it. And look for some general characteristics in the writers of snark.

A serious guess: Snark was born in a wash of boozy exuberance, perhaps in the eighth century B.C. Drawing on the work of classical scholars like Nancy Worman, in her recent study, *Abusive Mouths in Classical Athens,** we can create a myth of origins—the myth of snark. This much is known: In ancient Athens, aristocratic men gathered together at night to drink. Not exactly a surprise. They would put together a wine party, a symposium, that lasted the entire evening. (*Symposium,* one of Plato's greatest dialogues—a meditation on the nature of erotic and spiritual love—begins as a conventional drinking fest.) During these sloshed extravaganzas, the men entertained one another with stories, speeches, songs, and the like, until, on one such loosely strung occasion, a single reveler had the bright idea of taking the character of a lowborn Athenian. He assumed (as we would say) a persona—think of the elder President Bush in a toga suddenly becoming Billy Crystal or Andrew Dice Clay. Anyway, this licensed joker would abuse some chosen member of the party with many delicate reflections upon his mouth, his body parts, his manner of speaking, eating, and screwing. It was rather like a roast among show-business champions. As entertainment, it was crude, but the salient social point was that it took place within the walls or tents or around the fire of a club, and the humor of it depended on what I have called knowingness. If you didn't understand that a certain kind of joke was allowed, you wouldn't have been there in the first place. The insults were offered in a kind of lewd code that blessed those men privileged enough to hear it.

In the succeeding centuries, in the democratic era in Greece, rowdy assault burst out of the club walls and moved into the public arena. It moved into speech-making in the agora, or market-

* Cambridge University Press, 2008.

place, and in public squares, where it was identified as "invective" and pronounced in a formal style of vituperative poetry known as *iambos*. Yes, invective was a mode of poetry, a genre requiring certain metrical patterns and rhetorical modes, just like an elegy or a love lyric. You didn't just drop your turds in the street if you wanted to be taken seriously. The abuse was still what we might call snark, but it had to work *formally*.

In the agora, men known to the audience in the past as heroes or leaders were suddenly attacked. It was a startling development. Eventually, the comic assault moved elsewhere—into staged comedy, including the satyr plays, in which revelers and fornicators would bang one another on the head with giant phalluses (the satyr plays were a relief from the tragedies); it also moved, in the fifth century B.C., into the raffish satirical works of Aristophanes, some of which were lampoons of the famous laced with talk of farting, belching, and copulation. What makes all of this ragging activity, whether satirical or merely nasty, so much greater and more exhilarating than contemporary snark is the structured nature of the abuse: It was not only governed by compositional rules and standards, it was fully sustained—composed as a set of verses or as part of a play rather than as offhand remarks. These early versions of snark were also a risk-taking performance. If you offended a ruling power, you could be exiled or killed for it.

In the *iambos,* slander relied on denigration of the body. In particular, as Nancy Worman says, denigration of the mouth. The mouth was the appetitive organ, the consumer of feasts, the excesses of which were said to weaken the military fiber of Athens. The mouth was also a sexual instrument, giving pleasure to other men in a subservient position that was considered unmanly (the Greeks and Romans practiced and deplored homosexuality in bewildering combinations). Other orifices, of course, were put in play; in general, ancient snark reduced the body to its holes. Women, however, appear in this system of invective less as objects of lust than as figurative vessels of weakness, softness, or dissolute passion—that is, they were victimized by their own lust. In the beginning, snark was boy talk for boys. And, ever since, the male fear of female sexuality has been one of the recurring themes of snark; it remains that way even now. There are men all over the Web calling out to one another like wolves baying at the moon: "Women are *sluts.*"

In Greece, two poets in particular, Archilochus (born around 650 B.C.) and Hipponax (born maybe a hundred years later), became famous for their virtuosity in slanderous verse. The two masters have several things in common that are deliciously suggestive for the future history of their art. Archilochus was promised the hand of a highborn woman by her father. When the promise was withdrawn, Archilochus publicly pronounced *iambos* attacking his beloved as promiscuous and her father as a perjurer. A hundred years later, Hipponax, expelled by a local ruling tyrant, whom he had mocked in verse, set himself up in another city, where he was waylaid by two local sculptors who created his likeness—his likeness in stone as a deformed and malicious man. Hipponax took the same poetic revenge against his tormentors as Archilochus, and this is where the resemblance becomes uncanny: The victims of both poets committed suicide. Father and daughter and the two sculptors all hanged themselves. At least that's the story that the ancient Greeks believed, as reported by the Roman historian Pliny hundreds of years later. When I spoke to Professor Nancy Worman, she said that it was hard to say with certainty that the victims all committed suicide; she was sure, however, that if you wanted to be famous in ancient Greece as a writer of iambic poetry, you would be happy to have it known that your words were so powerful that the victims did away with themselves. By reputation, at least, the poets killed. How can W. H. Auden have said that poetry makes nothing happen?

The two poets were innovators in ways that enabled insult. They replaced the previous standard mode of epic hexameter, which was slow and measured—appropriate for elegy or praise of heroic warriors—with the faster, tighter iambic meter, which delivered abuse in quick, violent bursts. Their work is known today only in fragments. Archilochus' most famous line is, "For 'tis thy friends that make thee choke with rage." And then there is Hipponax's classic of misogyny, "There are two days when a woman is a pleasure: the day one marries her and the day one buries her." The fragments give us something of the acrid flavor. Consider the poets brilliant early practitioners of snark. And look at the pattern: First a wound of some sort, combined with a loss of standing or exile. Neither of these men had any power to begin with, and what dignity they had, in the way of citizenship, reputation, property, was taken away, their hopes destroyed. Then the revenge: They had become outsiders, but they took over the style of licensed lowbrow invective practiced earlier in the elite symposia, and formalized it into verse, which is easier to remember and to repeat than prose. What finally happened—or at least what they claimed happened—is wish fulfillment made flesh. Don't many writers of snark secretly hope that that their victims will crumple, collapse, and disappear? "For the snark *was* a Boojum, you see."

The myth of snark is complete.

Classical

Five hundred or so years later, Cicero, one of the great orators of the end of the Roman Republic, in the first century B.C., composed handbooks of rhetoric in which invective was a key element. In public-spirited Rome, you ascended by fighting well or speaking well, or both, and Cicero's handbooks were studied by aristocratic schoolboys. A political warrior himself, an enemy of Marc Antony, Cicero says that if you want to destroy your opponent, you have to sway the audience's emotions and appeal to its sense of the ridiculous. You demonize him by contrasting his vices with the ethical standards of the community—its appreciation of family lineage, courage, and character, the norms of aristocratic behavior. You can suggest all sorts of things about the victim's sex life, but you must use innuendo rather than outright obscenity ("monster" and "gelded pig" were among Cicero's actual epithets). For Cicero, as for the Greeks, the "impure mouth" was a major target. "You suck" was the essence of invective, and not entirely as a metaphor, either. Finally, the accusations flung at the opponent needn't be true. From the point of view of rhetorical effectiveness, telling the truth was less important than moving an audience to scorn.

In Rome, public life was strenuous, martial, noble, and, as you can see, fiercely abrasive. The arena was dangerous, but it could also present a series of opportunities for the ruthless. In 2004, Professor Christopher P. Craig, of the University of Tennessee, wrote an article on invective and its audience, assembling a list of the most frequently mentioned areas of personal vulnerability in Roman oratory. So here it is, Craig's List of Ancient Snark, a map of the turf, a feast, a gold mine. All potential snarkers, now shrinking in unworthy modesty, may harness their chariots and, with the authority of the Roman Senate behind them, feel free to attack the following: "1) embarrassing family origins; 2) being unworthy of one's family; 3) physical appearance; 4) eccentricity of dress; 5) gluttony and drunkenness, possibly leading to acts of *crudelitas* ("cruelty") and *libido* ("lust"); 6) hypocrisy in appearing virtuous; 7) avarice, sometimes linked with prodigality; 8) taking bribes; 9) pretentiousness; 10) sexual conduct; 11) hostility to one's family; 12) cowardice in war; 13) squandering one's patrimony, or financial embarrassment in general; 14) aspiring to *regnum* or tyranny, often associated with *vis* ("violence"), *libido, superbia* ("arrogance"), and *crudelitas;* 15) cruelty to citizens and allies; 16) plunder of private and public property; 17) oratorical ineptitude."

By my count, Bill Clinton was accused of all these things except eccentricity of dress and oratorical ineptitude, and George W. Bush was *guilty* of all these things except improper sexual conduct, taking bribes, and plundering government property. (Snark is irresistible at times.) Moving right along: What the list suggests is that the attributes of power-seeking men, and the way that others will attack them, has remained pretty much the same for two thousand years. But notice again the enormous difference between then and now: The rules in Rome were strict and formalized; if you wanted your rant to be taken seriously among the panegyrics and elegics and other forms of noble oratory, you attacked in a sustained and detailed way and within certain areas.

This much is clear: Someone who turns to snark always wants something else besides literary or rhetorical fame. The two Greek poets were seeking revenge; the Roman orators were seeking power. Snark is the expression of the alienated, of the ambitious, of the dispossessed. The history of classical-era abuse comes to a climax of sorts not in the speeches of a warrior-politician, but in the work of Juvenal, a sore-headed and much-aggrieved Roman poet who published sixteen "satires" in the first century A.D. Satire was a recognized genre in Rome, yet when reading Juvenal—which is quite an experience, rather like getting drunk during an obscene night in a comedy club—I wondered if *satire* was the right word for what he does. I wondered if the nature of his abuse, and everything in his life that produced it, didn't put him in the line of Archilochus and Hipponax as a writer of snark. Can't we claim Juvenal as snark's greatest talent, the peak from which every later version of the style seems a falling away?

Satire is derived from the Latin *satura lanx,* a "dish of fruits"—literally, a medley. The Romans invented the word and the genre—a literary medley, then, of high and low. (The word is not to be confused with the Greek word *satyr,* the name of the eternally erect and lascivious companion of the gods Pan and Dionysus.) The classical scholar Peter Green, in the introduction to his extraordinary translation of Juvenal,* notes that the Roman satirists Persius and Horace had tightened up the form of satire, making it orderly and concise, but that Juvenal's work was in line with the original notion of it as "a loose sequence of isolated scenes." And Juvenal has an astonishingly loose tone, too—ravaging, wildly embittered, cruelly funny. Is this really satire as we understand it?

When a flabby eunuch marries, when well-born girls go crazy
for pig-sticking up-country, bare-breasted, spear in fist;
when the barber who rasped away at my youthful beard has risen
to challenge good society with his millions; when Crispinus—
the Delta-bred house-slave, silt washed down by the Nile—
now hitches his shoulders under Tyrian purple, airs

* *The Sixteen Satires,* third edition. Penguin Books, 1998.

a thin gold ring in summer on his sweaty finger
("My dear, I couldn't bear *to wear my* heavier *jewels")—*
it's harder not *to be writing satires; for who could endure*
this monstrous city, however callous at heart, and swallow
   his wrath? (Satire I, 22–32)

In other words, Rome is so rotten, he has no choice but to
write in this way. But judging from the exuberance of his words,
I'm not sure he could have written in any other way. An im-
poverished landowner, Decimus Iunius Iuunalis, known as Juvenal, was born south of Rome around 55 A.D., a hundred years
after Cicero wrote his handbooks of rhetoric. As a young man,
Juvenal had enraged the whimsical and sadistic emperor Domitian. He recited an insult (he dared not write it down) aimed at
a court favorite—an actor, Paris, who controlled Domitian's the-
atrical and dance evenings. According to Juvenal, an aspiring
poet will "starve, unless he can sell his virgin libretto to Paris—
Paris, Director of Ballet, the jobber of high commands, who
hands out poets their six-month carpet-knighthoods." I suspect
there's an allusion to something dirty going on in that described
transaction (something like the casting couch), and Domitian, in
a kind of retaliatory practical joke, banished Juvenal to Egypt. In
the desert outpost, Juvenal suffered, among other humiliations,
the sight of Egyptians, who were colonial subjects, buying their
way into important jobs in the imperial administration. One of
these men, presumably, was the "Crispinus" of the excerpt
above.

When Domitian was assassinated (in 83 A.D.), the emperor
Nerva recalled Juvenal from his Egyptian mortification. Juvenal
then began issuing what eventually became the sixteen poems.
He attacked everyone. For instance, elderly homosexuals:

David Denby

Appearances are deceptive: every back street abounds
with solemn-faced humbuggers. You're castigating vice,
you, *the most notable dyke among all our Socratic fairies?*
Your shaggy limbs and the bristling hair on your forearms
proclaim a fierce spirit; but the surgeon who lances your swollen
piles beaks up at the sight of that well-smoothed passage.
    (Satire II, 8–13)

He also attacked the murdered emperor himself, who had im-
pregnated his niece and forced her to have an abortion ("and
every embryo stump was the living spit of Uncle"); literary pa-
trons whom he despised but depended on for an occasional meal
(he complained of the food); fast-fingered Greeks who were making a fortune in trade in the newly commercialized empire; the
rising children of freedmen or gladiators; the hustlers of both
sexes who haunted the banquet halls of the rich; aristocratic
women who had affairs with lower-class men (musicians, actors,
gladiators); indeed, women in general ("Don't you think it better
to sleep with a pretty boy?"). He attacked avarice and sensuality;
he attacked commercial activity—everything but soldiering, law-
yering, and farming.

As Peter Green has pointed out, Juvenal was devoted to the
notion of an unchanging Rome—the Rome of the late Republic,
before empire altered life forever. He was amazed that trade and
wealth had become as important as family lineage and inherited
property. Roman society, Juvenal wrote, was plagued by parvenus
showing off their recently acquired riches and by enfeebled aris-
tocrats who no longer had the morale to defend their own values;
instead, they wasted their patrimony in depravity and absurd lux-
uries. Very possibly the son of a freedman himself, Juvenal, like
some character in Shakespeare or Dickens, may have been tor-

mented by his own low birth. And, like Hipponax and Archilochus, he wanted vengeance, though in a convoluted way. An outsider with the values of an insider, he desperately needed to be admired by the aristocratic elite whose morals he slandered. He punished them, in effect, for not accepting him and giving him his due. His sense of loss and dispossession, and his chagrin over rising new wealth, sharpened anger into abuse.

I return to my question: Is Juvenal's work what we mean by satire? Or is it something else? I don't want to get caught in a thicket of definitions, so let me lay about quickly and brutally. Satire is always critical, directly or indirectly, of manners, vices, attitudes, persons, social types, or conditions. The satirist is enraged by what others accept. At its greatest, most powerful, and most dangerous, satire makes use of a double-edged sword—the devious and aggressive weapon of irony. The satirist practicing irony appears to praise the very thing he loathes. He exaggerates its features, and the terms of his praise give the show away. He tells truths in the form of lies.

Perhaps Juvenal can be seen a little more clearly by jumping forward for a moment to Jonathan Swift and Alexander Pope. In everyone's favorite example of high satire, Swift, reduced to despair by Ireland's poverty and feebleness, suggested, in "A Modest Proposal" (1729), that the poor address their economic difficulties by selling their children as food to the rich. Swift takes the tone of a reasonable social theorist and reformer, recommending a course of practical conduct. "A child will make two dishes as an entertainment for friends, and when the family dines alone the fore or hind quarter will make a reasonable dish, and seasoned with a little pepper or salt will be very good boiled on the fourth day, especially in winter." No personal attack here, no invective; the essay couldn't be more calm and orderly. "A Modest Proposal" is a series of eruptions whose effect on one's mind and emotions is way out of proportion to the quiet tone of the words on the page. Of course, that tone itself—smug, composed, all-knowing—was part of what Swift was making fun of. Another target is anyone who would allow Ireland to fall into its miserable state. We're meant to think that the rich, especially England's landed gentry, who controlled much of the turf and agriculture of Ireland, were *always* eating Ireland's children. For dry-ice contempt, Swift is incomparable. There's no trace of snark in "A Modest Proposal," but only what Swift called "savage indignation."

Irony is indirect yet aggressive, and potentially divisive. It can make people furious, since it splits the audience into those who get it and those who don't, and it sets up a hierarchy of wit between the two parties (you wouldn't want to spend time with anyone who read Swift's essay as a recipe for *fricassée enfantine*). It assaults the dunderheads who accept the dreadful conditions that are driving the satirist crazy, and it rewards the perceptive. In other words, satirical irony, by appealing to judgment, taste, and sensibility, is knowing not in the shallow way of snark but in the most serious way—it depends on the reader's critical intelligence and understanding, and perhaps his sense of tragedy. Irony assumes that God is laughing at you; snark assumes that your frat brothers are laughing *with* you. Irony can be ruthless and discriminatory—conservative, perhaps, in its values, but radical in its means.

Swift, in "A Modest Proposal," is untouchable, but other great satirists, in the midst of their art, may fall into snark now and then—the temptation can be irresistible. Swift's younger friend Alexander Pope created, in *The Dunciad,* from 1743, a mock epic poem devoted to the reign of Dullness, a goddess plenipotentiary who is systematically dousing the lights of wit and learning in

England. In passing, Pope "praises" many hack poets, but the special target of his raillery is the actor, playwright, theater manager, and poet laureate Colley Cibber, whom Pope crowns, with enormous fanfare, as the King of Dunces. Again, the note of personal chagrin, familiar from Juvenal: A few years earlier, Pope had ridiculed Cibber's verses, and Cibber had responded with a diatribe against Pope in pamphlet form in which, among other sallies, he joked about Pope's diminutive member as displayed in a whorehouse. Cibber was a popular man-about-town; Pope was four feet tall and a hunchback. As Samuel Johnson wrote, Pope "compared himself to a spider, and by another [writer] is described as protuberant behind and before." Yet this misshapen, embittered, and sickly genius had many friends who admired and feared his wit. Parts of the extraordinary *Dunciad* may have been intended as snarky malice for literary workers and readers in the capital who shared Pope's slighting views of Cibber:

Swearing and supperless the Hero sate,
Blasphemed the Gods, the Dice, and damn'd his Fate;
Then gnaw'd his pen, then dashed it on the ground,
Sinking from thought to thought, a vast profound!
Plung'd for his sense, but found no bottom there;
Yet wrote and flounder'd on in mere despair.
Around him much Embryo, much Abortion lay,
Much future Ode, and abdicated Play;
Nonsense precipitate, like running Lead,
That slipped thro' Cracks and Zig-zags of the Head;
All that on Folly Frenzy could beget,
Fruits of dull Heat, and Sooterkins of Wit.
Next, o'er his Books his eyes began to roll,
In pleasing memory of all he stole,

David Denby

How here he sipp'd, how there he plunder'd snug,
And suck'd all o'er, like an industrious Bug. (Book II, 115–130)

This is brilliant but also cruel and vindictive. The mock-heroic frame of *The Dunciad,* with its magnificent lofty Miltonic cadences and its sudden plunges into abysses of contempt ("like an industrious Bug"), is dazzling satiric composition. But Pope mixes base metals with gold: He monumentalized caricature, and harped on works by Cibber that had never appeared (Cibber, as suggested above, had abandoned some of his more ambitious plays). He attacked poets and dramatists ("lull'd by soft Zephyrs thro' the broken pane") who were merely poor—that is, writers who were not gentlemen with inherited wealth, and who wrote plays or verse to make a living. He settles scores with rival poets and attacks men in literary London who have received praise. I'm not saying that vengeance was Pope's sole or sufficient motive (he is, in *The Dunciad,* a critic and celebrator of literature as well as a great poet), but chagrin and spiteful retort were central to the genesis of the poem's composition,* and many of the personal comments are poisoned shafts, insinuating, mean, and low. In the end, the mighty *Dunciad* structure seems too grand by half—a flame-breathing dragon stomping on toads—and, as you read it, you feel slightly unclean for having been caught in the toils of Pope's malevolence. So even the greatest satirist can descend, in part of his work, to snark.

With these two formidable eighteenth-century examples in mind, we can see more easily where Juvenal stands. In the hier-

---

* There was an earlier version of *The Dunciad,* from 1728, in which a different rival, Lewis Theobald, was the chief target. Theobald had brought out a book in 1726 suggesting that Pope's edition of Shakespeare's works was full of errors and inconsistent practices. Pope retaliated.

archy of wit, Swift, the practitioner of snark-free momentous irony in "A Modest Proposal," is at the top; Pope the malignant genius is down from the summit a bit; and Juvenal, though still a great writer, down still further.

How can one have anything but mixed feelings about Juvenal? He wrote his verses in formal meter—dactylic hexameter—and in a recognized genre. But satire, in our sense of the word, requires more than invective and vituperation; it requires the dramatized or implied belief in some outraged ideal, some better way of life or art than the fallen and degraded versions that the satirist attacks. And denunciation of vices doesn't, by itself, put one in the exclusive circle, either. The satirist, trying to cleanse the world of its ills, praises some corresponding set of virtues, even if only by implication (Pope's rhetorical grandeur invokes a world of epic heroes, and, in passing, he praises Rabelais, Shakespeare, and Swift). Juvenal is critical, God knows, but no one could call his rage cleansing. When he attempts praise of an alternate way of life—a golden age of early Rome, when men were men, and women were "chaste"—he's not at all convincing. His encomiums to a mythical past seem slyly absurd, even farcical. What's convincing is Juvenal's stunning viciousness about the present. The energy is all negative.

Along with Horace, Persius, and Petronius, he receives high honors in the standard studies of classical satire, but why not tell the truth and say that he's less a satirist than a genius of snark, the absolute master of teasing, filthy, misogynist, undermining insult? He's an invincible entertainer; he makes you want to hear more and more of his badinage—another outrage, another piece of ridiculous behavior! He depends on the reliable fear of women's sexuality. Have you heard that Messalina, the emperor Claudius's wife, would arise from the emperor's bed, call "for her hooded night-cloak," and make straight "for her brothel, with its stale, warm coverlets"? The charge was nonsensical—sheer sexual loathing and male paranoia. But listen to the writer's voice:

> *She would greet each client sweetly, demand cash payment,*
> *and absorb all their battering—without ever getting up.*
> *Too soon the brothel-keeper dismissed his girls:*
> *she stayed right till the end, always the last to go,*
> *then trailed away sadly, still with burning, rigid vulva,*
> *exhausted by men, yet a long way from satisfied,*
> *cheeks grimed with lamp smoke, filthy, carrying home*
> *to her Imperial couch the stink of the whorehouse.*

This may be obscene, but it's also literature, and its narrative and figurative power produce an uncanny effect: Juvenal slanders Messalina so extravagantly that the poet breaks through, so to speak, to the other side of snark. He pushes the absurd charges so far, and with such compositional brilliance, that he winds up turning Messalina into a kind of heroine. In this case, snark creates a champion, a gladiator of eros.

Reading Juvenal convinced me that invective at its utmost pitch of fury—sustained and unrelenting, and formally composed—can amount to something great. It may be a lesser form than satire, but, at its best, it is very far from nothing. The trouble with today's snarky pipsqueaks who break off a sentence or two, or who write a couple of mean paragraphs, is that they don't go far enough; they don't have a coherent view of life. Spinning around in the media from moment to moment, they don't stand for anything, push for anything; they're mere opportunists without dedication, and they don't win any victories. For Juvenal's enemies disappeared, too. It's very likely that he had nothing to do with it, but, still, the Paris that he ridiculed—Domitian's favorite—was executed. He was killed, of course, on Domitian's orders, and then, a few years later, the emperor who had banished Juvenal to Egypt was murdered himself. In the end, both enemies vanished. "For the snark *was* a Boojum, you see."

———

These few classic examples suggest a dynamic model of snark. It may flare up when a personal wound has festered, when a writer is physically miserable and mocked, when he has been exiled or dispossessed or passed over. The excruciations of envy, suffering pride, and damaged amour propre drive the writer low. And snark is most likely to flow when one of two complementary social conditions is present: First, when a dying class of the powerful, or would-be powerful, struggles to keep the barbarians from entering the hallowed halls. Juvenal, paradoxically, was an outsider who never questioned the values of the insiders; he merely demanded that they hold on to what they believed in. (Late in Juvenal's life, the emperor Hadrian settled an income on him, and his tone grew milder. He had joined the elite at last.) That's one type of snarker—the instinctive Tory, the reactionary holding to a fixed order. (Pope hated the writers who turned literature into a mere *trade*.) But snark may also be the weapon of outsiders who want to displace the insiders, who want to take over the halls of the powerful and expel the officeholders. In certain periods, when new people are socially empowered to write, speak, and judge, and writing is the vessel of social ambition, snark becomes more than likely. When such a shift is combined with the development of new reading and writing technologies, like the Internet, snark becomes inevitable.

A Brief, Highly Intermittent History of Snark, Part 2

In which the author brings his search almost to the present era, celebrating and deploring certain publications and exposing the snarky tendencies of a famous author.

The Near Past

Hunting the snark is a fine adventure, but I'm not eager to try the reader's patience in an exhaustive search. It's the perfected and powerful examples, the fools of snark and its occasional heroes, who interest me the most. In this little survey, I've obviously skipped a lot, and I now jump over the other classical-era practitioners, the lesser British wits of the eighteenth century, over Evelyn Waugh in the 1920s, too, and finally over all the snarling pamphleteers and political broadside writers in both Great Britain and America—jumping all the way, in fact, to the early sixties in England, when a bunch of raffish Oxford graduates created a satirical rag, *Private Eye,* using a new process known as "photolitho offset." What this process enabled was a clumsy precursor of blogging: Suddenly anyone could start a magazine.

A significant part of the core group among the founders had known one another at the Shrewsbury School in Shropshire, which had a humor magazine then called *The Wallopian* (later it was called *The Fallopian,* signifying, I suppose, a shift from punishment to creation). I think you could safely say that the boys, including Richard Ingrams, Willie Rushton, Christopher Booker, and Paul Foot, as well as other collaborators picked up at Oxford, shared certain aesthetic tastes which did not extend to an appreciation of visual beauty. Launched in 1961, a great period for popular satire in Britain,* *Private Eye* was irregularly typed and pasted up; it was printed in varying shades of sepulchral black and gray. It looked a fright, but it was potent in its slovenliness—the ultimate summer-camp mimeo, with drawings by the young Ralph Steadman, who later became famous in America as Hunter S. Thompson's illustrator, and Gerald Scarfe, who has had a long career on both sides of the Atlantic as a cartoonist and artist.

In the earliest issues, the editors' recent attendance at school couldn't be missed. Undergraduate snarls like the following exam question turned up:

EXTRA CONSTITUTIONAL LAW, PART 1

Draft a Mixed Race Sexual Relations Act making it legal to rape but not to marry a white woman. Explain the various positions of a Japanese.

This sally, I think—I would *like* to think—is satire of miscegenation laws that forbade marriage between the races at a time in which (in the American South, at least) no white man had ever

---

* The satirical review *Beyond the Fringe* got going in 1960, and the mock TV-news show *That Was the Week That Was* started up in 1962.

been prosecuted for raping a black woman. It's an ironic joke, then—and not snarky—which turns a real situation on its head. If I sound a little unsure, that's because some of the jokes in *Private Eye* are simply racist, without any ironic twist. Consider the situation of the editors of *Private Eye* in 1961—educated, upper-middle-class and upper-class young white men putting out a humor magazine at the end of an extraordinary imperial run. By the sixties, Britain was rapidly losing the rest of the empire that it had begun losing at the end of World War II. Ghana, Nigeria, Sierra Leone, and many other British colonies had just declared independence or would declare it very soon. Increasingly, the nonwhite world claimed sovereignty, a situation that did not inspire the editors and writers with the most generous emotions. An early issue featured a cartoon of two liberated Africans in robes, one wearing a crown, the other an English bowler. The caption read as follows: "There are some jobs which are better left to the whites . . ." The mixture of contempt and self-contempt in that cartoon—a mood of imperialist chagrin—is startling, perhaps unprecedented.

At the same time, however, that British power was rapidly fading in the great world, there was a regnant establishment at home—royalty, church, government, press lords, labor bosses, famous journalists and intellectuals, all of them going about their business with a stern authority of manner. They were ripe for taking down, and *Private Eye* burlesqued such targets as inept and corrupt pols, government organs that did not function, and sclerotic newspapers (subscription request: "Please send me the Sunday *Telegraph*. I am dead"). The magazine teased young men on the make who shamelessly fawned over power; it attacked nepotism among the upper classes ("Merryman Tube has just come down from Cambridge, and has already had 17 novels published by the avant-garde house of Rupture and Tube"); it regularly hauled out such farcical favorites as scandal-hunting policemen, known by the single name of "Inspector Knacker of the Yard." (The Yard was Scotland Yard; "knackers" was Brit slang for *balls* and also the name for worn-out horses ready to be put down.)

Private Eye was, and is (it's still going), consistently funny in a bright, larking, eternal-schoolboy sort of way. It turned loose a battalion of silly names; it spoofed the rigidities of British class structures and manners, always in tight, rhythmically charged little sentences that released their venom without losing their composure. The audience was educated enough to pick up the references and share in the exhilaration of contempt—a perfect situation for snark. Still, reading the early issues now, one feels the uneasiness behind the high and low nonsense. Like Juvenal, the *Private Eye* gang had a ruling-class mentality without a ruling-class portfolio. In terms of authority, they were outsiders, but their values were strictly those of the insiders—but insiders whose position in the great world had diminished. The attitude of the magazine was paradoxical: "We are defeated, but everyone else is ridiculous. We have no power, but we will win this game through the strength of our disdain."

Caught in this ambivalent state—both wounded and aggressive—the magazine was promiscuous in its appetite for ridicule. The editors made fun of complacent, reactionary members of Parliament in the created personage of "Sir Bufton Tufton," who resided in the imaginary country town of Lymeswold. Yet the editors' own tastes were often miffed, exasperated, blighted, mischievously bigoted. Snark fell like manna into knowing ears. The kind of squeamishness that Americans increasingly felt about attacking vulnerable racial and sexual minorities was nonexistent in ruling-class Britain, where neither men nor women were known for their politeness to the Irish, to the Jews, or to persons of dusky hue. In *Private Eye*, Asians, blacks, and homosexuals ("pooves") got banged about the ears. So did the lower orders in general; and so did Jews, especially billionaire parvenu Jews like Sir Robert Maxwell ("Cap'n Bob") and Sir James Goldsmith ("Sir Jammy Fishpaste"). All these people were obnoxious, absurd, out of the question; so was the triumphant military state of Israel, known repeatedly, and without fondness, as "plucky little Israel." Palestine may have been a pain in the neck for the British, but they had ruled it from 1920 to 1948, and it was gone. The *Private Eye* boys had not been exiled, but they had certainly been dispossessed, and, for them, Great Power doings were now just silly. *Private Eye* snarked the Bay of Pigs mess with spoofed reports about the Cuban resistance ("bearded little faggots"), and, much later, it yawned over the fall of the Berlin Wall—the celebration was "the most boring ceremony of the decade."

Snark, by its very nature, is philistine; it will never honor the artistically and intellectually ambitious, who see the world as a field of ravishing possibilities or as tragedy. Writers of snark see the world as a series of false appearances. What else can snarky writers do but repeat their obsessions? If they give up the relentless attack on hypocrisy and pomposity (which is often just money and success), they would be weaponless. In order to regain their edge, they would have to elevate their work to the level of intellectual satire, which is a lot harder to write. Snark, in general, is not given to hard work. Written by intellectuals, but infuriated by intellect at its most ambitious, *Private Eye* penned up the seriously serious in a reader-generated feature called "Pseuds Corner," in which philosophical and artistic eminences were quoted as pretentious fools—Jean-Paul Sartre and other Frenchmen were particular favorites. In an astounding mistake, *Private Eye*, which was indifferent to pop culture in general, persistently nagged at the Beatles, whom it dubbed "the Turds." (Other pop groups later acquired the same honorary name.) In 1967, the magazine reviewed the revolutionary album *Sgt. Pepper's Lonely Hearts Club Band,* with its startling layered and textured sound, as follows:

> *For the Turds the wailing noise marks a new departure. Their latest L.P., "A Day in the Life of Ex-King Zog of Albania," took over five years to make and includes combs on paper, the sound of the Cornish Riviera Express leaving Paddington Station, two million zithers, an electric hydrofoil and the massed strings of the Tel Aviv Police band.*

Funny enough, and the Beatles certainly were not hard up for cash or critical support. But, really—the *Beatles*? At what point is spoof no longer naughty but just out of it? Snark's aesthetic judgments can't be trusted; it has too modest a rooting interest in artists actually succeeding at anything. The magazine pulled down the knickers of the great Virginia Woolf, and cut up Britain's most accomplished contemporary artists, including the Kitchen Sink school of novelists, who wrote about angry young men in the working-class Midlands and other such unimaginable places (" 'A Pride of Snoggings,' Bernard Flan's new novel, tells the story of William Dudd, an unskilled laborer in a shoe shop in a town somewhere in the North of England . . .").

Private Eye is more endearing when it leaves art alone and teases the British libel laws with its patented euphemisms— "Ugandan discussions" for public sexual misadventures; "tired and emotional" for persons sloppily drunk at the wrong time; and "exotic cheroot" for whatever weed famous people smoked when they weren't smoking tobacco. In *Private Eye*'s mock attacks, the insults and coded speech of the old Athenian drinking associations had flowered into entertainment for an expansive club composed of the readers—but no more than the readers (the magazine is fairly impenetrable to the uninitiated). As far as *Private Eye* was concerned, effectiveness at creating scandal counted far more than truth (despite the euphemisms, the magazine was successfully sued for libel on a number of occasions). Accurate or not, *Private Eye*'s snark was the revenge of the dispossessed on the world. The writers and editors couldn't run things, but at least they could scrawl on the facade of power, disrupt the official narrative of how England worked.

Did the heartlessly funny snark of *Private Eye* ever do anyone in? Sir Robert Maxwell (Cap'n Bob), the Czech-born Holocaust survivor who became, in Great Britain, an entrepreneur, media lord, and big-time scoundrel, successfully sued the magazine for libel, and was paid £225,000. (At the time, the editor, Ian Hislop, said, "I've just given a fat cheque to a fat Czech."). Yet some years later, in 1991, Cap'n Bob, then in disgrace, died absurdly by falling off his luxury yacht and drowning in the sea. The Boojum, it seems, had struck again.

———

The snark of *Private Eye* was produced by young men suffering from a grievously injured and ambiguous national inheritance—an elite attacking an older elite that had lost power. By contrast, the derision that Tom Wolfe launched in his famous *New York* magazine article "These Radical Chic Evenings," in 1970, was aimed at an American elite unwilling simply to settle for the power that it had earned. Wolfe's article* re-created a notorious

* It was republished in 1970 in a book with another essay on a similar theme, "Mau-Mauing the Flak Catchers."

Manhattan party in 1969 in which rich, Jewish show-business celebrities, including Leonard Bernstein, Barbara Walters, and the movie directors Sidney Lumet and Otto Preminger, attempted to help what they took to be a threatened minority. In their thirteen-room Park Avenue duplex apartment, the conductor and composer Leonard Bernstein and his actress-socialite wife Felicia Montealegre threw a fund-raiser for the Black Panthers. Indicted on charges that included conspiring to bomb various sites in New York and to kill police officers, the "Panther 21," as they were called, were something of a civil-liberties cause. Many people besides the Bernsteins and their guests wondered whether the Panthers had been set up by the FBI. (In 1971, the Panther 21 group was acquitted of all charges in the case.) But the Bernstein party took place in a luxurious milieu during "the season of radical chic," as Wolfe called it, and the piece Wolfe wrote about it became a "classic" which, today, almost forty years later, reads less like a classic than like a foundational document in the development of American snark.

Wolfe's compositional resources seem to me as spectacular as ever. With inordinate ease, he passes in and out of the heads of various participants, describes the manners and clothes and voices, the hors d'oeuvres and decor and other social furnishings with what feels like dead-on accuracy and glinting malice. Wolfe is a master of snarky mimesis, the reenactment of mood and point of view:

> *Deny it if you wish to, but such are the* pensées métaphysiques *that rush through one's head on those Radical Chic evenings just now in New York. For example, does that huge Black Panther there in the hallway, the one shaking hands with Felicia Bernstein herself, the one with the black leather coat and*

the dark glasses and the absolutely unbelievable Afro, Fuzzy-
Wuzzy scale, in fact—is he, a Black Panther, going to pick up
the Roquefort cheese morsel rolled in crushed nuts from off the
tray, from a maid in uniform, and just pop it down the gullet
without so much as missing a beat of Felicia's perfect Mary
Astor voice . . .

It's a terrific joke that the Bernsteins and other East Side hosts, so as not to offend the Panthers, had to scramble to find servants who were white. In his principal thrust, Wolfe certainly drew blood: He accused the fashionable guests of what he called double-tracking; that is, of wanting to hold on to their high position, wealth, and prerogatives and, at the same time, to undergo the exciting, socially advanced experience of meeting black revolutionaries in leather and shades who talked menacingly of guns and of overthrowing "the system." The spectacle of East Side chic hosting the Panthers was, as Wolfe repeatedly says, "delicious" in its incongruities. And his teasing, taunting sentences, copious, fluent, all-encompassing, create a lilt of absurdity in which commonplace remarks, and even sensible remarks, seem weirdly funny.

The element that lowers Wolfe's writing from social satire to snark is his contempt for absolutely everyone. "Radical Chic" is not animated by the satirist's sharp, outraged, correcting desire for a better world. There's no ironic suggestion of a paradise lost, of finer values than what's on display. Swift thought Ireland was at stake; Pope thought literature was at stake. I don't mean to suggest that the future of a country or an art form are the only subjects grand enough to inspire satire, but what was at stake for Wolfe? When he talked about "New Society" as a group that sets values in the New York beau monde, he meant those who had big money, and mostly *new* big money. If he meant to set them off against an earlier WASP elite, he didn't say so. But with no conceivable current standard that he admired, Wolfe had nothing to fall back on but his comic catalog of poor taste and his own superiority as an untouchable observer—an observer who was never implicated in anything he reported. Famously, Wolfe invariably wore a white suit, cultivating the mask of the dandy and the grandee, a conscious anachronism out of the Old South or perhaps the hedonistic, moneyed side of the twenties. Wolfe's dandy getup, at first a brilliant piece of bravado, finally seemed a curiosity whose meanings never expanded beyond the early registration of it as an ironic joke. If Wolfe, in his white suit, didn't want to be touched or dirtied by anything, that was his problem, not a comment on America.

In his exuberant derision, Wolfe lacked even elementary moral curiosity. He certainly had little sympathy for the liberal Jews who, no matter how successful, still had tribal memories of oppression fresh enough to cause them to rally to the side of what they assumed was a threatened minority, the Black Panthers; nor had Wolfe any interest in the civil rights movement in any form. A "Black Panther" with his "Fuzzy-Wuzzy" was nothing more than an exotic amusement for him, a fashionable thug on display in an East Side living room. But, in the same essay, he made it clear that the established, older generation of black civil rights leadership was ridiculous, too:

> *For many years Jewish members of New Society have supported such organizations as NAACP, the Urban League, and CORE. And no doubt they have been sincere about it, because the organizations have never had much social cachet; i.e., they have had "middle class" written all over them. All one had to do was look at the "Negro leaders" involved. There they were, up on*

the dais at the big hotel banquet, wearing their white shirts, their Hart, Schaffner & Marx suits three sizes too big, and their academic solemnity.

Forty years ago, Hart, Schaffner & Marx was the chain store you went to when you had no more than seventy-five bucks for a suit. Those men in their ill-fitting suits were American heroes to the core; you might say they had the right stuff. And two grains of sympathy would have suggested to Wolfe that men who had never had much power in the past would want to appear as respectable as possible. In Wolfe, judgment always comes down to a snarky comedy of accessories: You are what you wear.

The joke, however, is on Wolfe. Brilliantly composed as it is, "Radical Chic" now seems more fatuous than the assembled partygoers. Wolfe may have thought them absurd, but the concerned wealthy liberals Bernstein and Barbara Walters, and also rude Otto Preminger, tried to talk sense to the "revolutionary" Panthers that night; they tried to argue them out of their fantasies of violence, and, at this point, the slumming celebrities seem no sillier than other well-meaning people dedicated to a hopeless mission. Apart from their partying over a civil-liberties case, how foolish *were* they? Wolfe even quotes Leonard Bernstein saying, sometime after the party, "If we deny these Black Panthers their democratic rights because their philosophy is unacceptable to us, then we are denying our own democracy," which sounds like the sternly honorable words of a civil libertarian, not the lamely fashionable sentiment of the dummy whom Wolfe ridicules in the rest of the piece.

For Tom Wolfe, writing "Radical Chic" may have marked a turning point. In his early books, Wolfe was the ebullient chronicler of hippies and custom-car fanciers and other wild-ass exuberant outliers in the great circus of American pop culture. After "Radical Chic," he wrote a fine, ultrasquare book about the American astronauts, *The Right Stuff* (1979), and a fascinating novel about the fools of eighties finance capitalism, *The Bonfire of the Vanities* (1987)—fascinating, and depressing, among other reasons, for the ridicule he poured on a variety of black characters on the edge of the action. Wolfe then became a rather sour neocon, apostle to the op-ed page of the *Wall Street Journal* and the conservative think tank the Manhattan Institute. Perhaps the Bernstein party was just one sixties event too many for him, and he retreated from celebration to a disdain that had always been there. In the end, that white suit may have been less an ironic joke than the heraldic uniform of a man born in Richmond, Virginia, who entertained fancies of a distinguished Old South in which blacks kept their mouths shut, a conservative who had never accustomed himself to the new money in the Northeast. Of course, Wolfe lived in New York and became the toast of the town; the Northeast rich, at least the conservative division, welcomed him into their fold. Unlike Juvenal, he probably had little cultural respect for the elites whose approval he evidently craved. In brief, Tom Wolfe's life got swallowed up by irony. Snark as a habit of contemptuous low wit brought Tom Wolfe out—or rather, it lured him into an unhappy, jeering corner that he has never since left.

The Seed of the Present

Tom Wolfe was a key transmission point between the unyielding giggle and crow of *Private Eye* and the assorted minor outrages of *Spy,* the center of American snark in the eighties. *Spy,* too, relished the "delicious" social incongruities of New York social life. The magazine's two founding editors, Graydon Carter and Kurt

Andersen, were both young men from outside the city—Carter came from the Ottawa suburbs, Andersen from Omaha, Nebraska—and both arrived with richly burnished fantasies of the metropolis. Manhattan was money and status, glamour and dirt, art and infamy. It was corrupt, even criminal, and it was run according to a series of mystiques that no one actually understood. Filthy deals and hidden arrangements by day, a saturnalia of dinner parties, galas, and clubs at night! Desperately ambitious socialites and outrageous hangers-on! A true demimonde! As the editors reimagined New York, the city was a kind of usable fiction—a journalist's created paradise—and *Spy* became almost touching in its desire that the city live up to the perfervid notion that its editors had of it. In order to get going, the editors raised money mostly from the younger members of wealthy families—trust-fund babies with cash to burn, men unafraid of punishment. What tone to use for their sportive new magazine? Carter and Andersen took certain elements from the early (1920s) versions of the *New Yorker* and *Vanity Fair,* and also from *Esquire*'s habit in the sixties of tagging hot writers and cultural fashions—except that *Spy* was not debonair like the first two magazines, nor in love with literature like the last. Manhattan was *wicked,* and the right tone to capture its wickedness had to be acrid, knowing, and both undermining and caressing at once.

The editors wanted to find out where the power was, though their fascination was severely limited in range. Finance and the media—especially inside trading on Wall Street and the workings of such prestige publications as the *Times,* the *New Yorker,* the Condé Nast empire of magazines—obsessed them, but such major industries and power centers in the city as politics, law, the universities, advertising, and medicine left them pretty much cold. *Spy* was a guide less to power in New York than to a young journalist's or financial worker's desire to *gain* power in New York. The club of knowing readers consisted of avid young locals eager to grab the brass ring and (later) out-of-towners who enjoyed seeing New York's celebrities put down as a bunch of grubby fools. "JERKS: The Ten Most Embarrassing New Yorkers" was the cover story in the first issue (October 1986). The editors were so excited by what they had to say about the city that the body type, in clashing fonts, rushed right to the edges of the page—a little like frantic Manhattan itself, which, overdeveloped and airless, spills to the borders of the Hudson and the East River.

The name of the magazine was partly derived from the old Katharine Hepburn–Cary Grant movie *The Philadelphia Story* (1940), in which a scurrilous publication called *Spy* orders its reporters to penetrate the great houses and wedding parties of the superrich. Playwright Philip Barry and screenwriter Donald Ogden Stewart (who did the movie adaptation of Barry's stage success) were writing about old American money—the mainline WASPs genuinely eager to guard their privacy. But in New York, in the eighties, celebrities and Wall Street entrepreneurs lived a good part of their lives in public. Many of them not only welcomed attention, they thrived on it, and *Spy* was more than ready to pay heed. No matter how nasty the magazine became in its teasing of what it later called "mummified boulevardiers [i.e., gossip columnist Liz Smith], socialite war criminals [Henry Kissinger], beaver-faced moguls [Barry Diller, Michael Ovitz], tigress survivors [any one of a dozen East Side socialites], and, of course, short-fingered vulgarians [Donald Trump and other plutocrats]," *Spy* remained the celebrities' snarling little doggie, lovable for its growls and snapping teeth.*

---

* This descriptive line is taken from the exceptionally self-approving commemorative volume *Spy: The Funny Years*. Miramax, 2006.

The editors were irreverent toward persons—the tone was physically intimate and coarse—but never toward power or money itself, which *Spy* took very seriously indeed. *Spy* was snark composed for beginners who needed to master the right insouciant style and avoid foolish errors. There's nothing wrong with that—every rising generation requires instruction in attitude—but the notion that the magazine was, as some people naively thought, "antiestablishment," or, as the editors later put it, "a little dangerous," was quite absurd. (Growling dogs don't need to be muzzled; they need to be fed.) *Spy,* unlike vengeful Hipponax and other snarkers, did not want its victims to disappear. It wanted them to hang around so they could be attacked again and again. The magazine and its subjects were mutually dependent on each other.

Spy excelled at mapping, laying out the turf. It published endless lists of who mattered and who didn't, who was a crook and who might soon be heading for the slammer. It reveled in actual drawings of power's physical arrangements, its disposition in space. Mapping, it turned out, was *Spy*'s version of investigative reporting. The magazine made a diagram of where everyone sat at lunch in the Russian Tea Room, Manhattan's blini-and-caviar gathering place in the late eighties for top-ranked movie executives, actors, and agents. It penetrated Bohemian Grove—the Northern California redwoods retreat of conservative politicians and corporation leaders—and charted where Kissinger, George Schultz, the Bushes, and other notables drank and peed and slept when they were there. It also assembled a complete list of the clients of Creative Artists Agency, the Hollywood agency run by the (then) omnipotent Michael Ovitz. This grand act of mapping was a genuine service to students of the movie business. CAA specialized in the practice of packaging talent—their own clients—and then negotiating brutally with the movie studios in ways that helped the agency but may have screwed up the movies that emerged from the package. One needed to know who those clients were.

But mapping also has a number of purely snarky functions. First of all, it said to the powerful: We *see* you. We're getting inside your doors, inside your heads. We will penetrate your secrets and embarrass you. *Spy*'s snarky version of investigative reporting included such pranks as listing the parking tickets accumulated by major New York corporations and institutions. The magazine counted how often celebrities had actually voted in recent elections. The malicious rug-pulling was fun to watch, but there was also something creepy, parasitic, and finally meaningless about such minor invasions. *Spy* never did find out how power worked in New York or what deals between political and corporate honchos were struck in Bohemian Grove; it discovered only where power hung out and what its vulgar habits were. Snark, in the end, is investigative reporting's bastard, weak-limbed child. And this odd desire to get *inside* the buildings—wasn't it, in its parodistic way, a kind of rehearsal for legitimate entry? *Spy* practiced snark imperiously, as a loud rap on the door. I see you; I insult you; I am you. The magazine instructed its readers on how to penetrate the money culture while preserving the right attitude of superiority to it.

There's a second purely snarky function of mapping: It tells you whom you can safely put down—who sits at the wrong table or is banned at the door. *Spy* tabbed the obvious losers, running, for instance, a nauseating piece that deplored the way Puerto Ricans and other poor Latino immigrants in New York failed to speak proper Castilian Spanish. This outbreak of class and race snobbery was unusual for the magazine, which generally treated the poor as invisible. More typically, *Spy* was eager to locate, list, and ridicule worn-out elites—"has-beens" and "coasters" who had done something once and had allegedly drifted in their careers ever since. In the philistine tradition of snark, the magazine, as if working for Hollywood moguls, noted that movies starring such greats as Meryl Streep and Robert De Niro had not actually made much money. They were losers, too. The magazine judged everyone—this person was "appalling," that one "loathsome"—as if imposing a label were some fearless act of social criticism. Most of *Spy*'s negative judgments about people (and there weren't many positive ones) were moralized versions of personal distaste. Like Wolfe, the editors and writers despised the greedy new rich, though, again like Wolfe, apart from a few faded copies of the old *Vanity Fair,* they had no golden age as a source of nostalgia and achievement to appeal to. Satire depends on "shared norms" (as the sociologists put it), and the only shared norm in New York was money. The corrective standard, presumably, was people who spent their money tastefully, but where was the journalistic interest in that? *Spy* had to go low and stay low merely to exist:

> *Ferret-eyed snitch Ivan Boesky* [a convicted Wall Street inside trader] *has three limousines to convey him from his tacky, expensive Westchester estate to his suite of expensive, tacky offices at 650 Fifth Avenue. Two-thirds of the motorcade is bogus—decoys, presumably, so that hit-men, finked-on former colleagues and flower-vending Moonies won't know which one contains the disgraced arbitrageur.*

I can think of only one time that *Spy* appealed to nature rather than to taste, and that article, in its startling shift of focus, was one of the best pieces of snark the magazine ever

David Denby

published. In March 1987, *Spy* ran a photo spread ("Too Rich & Too Thin") devoted to the wealthy society women in Manhattan who were starving themselves so they could squeeze into their evening dresses. The photographs highlighted aged necks and hands, and the accompanying text, by Nell Scovell, was cruel:

> *In New York there is an inverse relationship between a woman's dress size and the size of her apartment. A size 2 gets a 14 room apartment. A size 14 gets a 2 room apartment . . . Rubenesque heft on a woman used to be a sure sign of wealth, as only the rich could afford to eat well. At Le Cirque these days, the ladies who lunch play with their $28 prix fixe meals and come out thinner than when they went in. Miraculously, even those who like to eat seem not to gain weight. (In fact, one moneyed scarecrow donates her soiled coiffure castoffs to the Metropolitan Museum's Costume Institute. Soiled, says an Institute source, not with sweat or champagne, but with vomit.)*

> *Such emaciation is worth nothing if it is not flaunted: diamond chokers clasp chicken necks, Chanel chains bind boyish hips, emeralds droop from shriveled earlobes. And doesn't it seem that the more the wife diets, the more the husband balloons? . . . Evenings, the couples march off to black-tie affairs looking like Olive Oyl and Bluto.*

Perfectly phrased, with a witty use of alliteration, and also spiced with a touch of social conscience. All in all, it's as good, in its way, as Juvenal.

What did this monthly outpouring of snark amount to? *Spy*'s habit of mapping and grading expressed a genuine New York Terror—the fear that one wouldn't know enough to qualify, that one was gauche or (*Spy*'s favorite word) "clueless." Gaining approval in New York's glamour occupations was infinitely treacherous. Culture, family, tradition—none of this really meant very much. You had very little to rely on. There was only your nimble-footed, infinitely changeable readiness to size up the field, and to take advantage of an opening. And once you had made it, you had to continue making it—either that, or become a "coaster." At the least, if you were knowingly tart, you could appease the Terror by appearing up-to-date or even ahead of an ever-fluctuating notion of taste. You signaled your momentary mastery of the flux by putting down some famous person—Norman Mailer, say. That Mailer had a long record of achievement as well as a long record of foolishness was beside the point. Justice was hardly the issue. Snark was a means of survival on competitive turf.

Well, ease up. The magazine didn't live long (only five years in its prime state), and, in its brief life, it created a party atmosphere, an air of flash and swank and popping corks. *Spy* was literate and resourceful; it did odd, funny things, and in its articles, say, on fashionable consumerism—designer teakettles and the like ("Yuppie Porn")—it mocked the habits of its own readers, which took some courage. Many of its editors and writers went on to successful careers in other magazines or in television, and the magazine's tone and style—the brief paragraphs in clashing type fonts, the charts and lists, the sarcasm and media-hip allusiveness—poured into other publications and into late-night-TV comedy and many other things. *Spy*'s legacy is mixed at best, but one can't blame the degeneracy of most contemporary snark on *Spy*'s editors and contributors.

The hunt through history is now over, and I must turn, with sorrowful steps, toward today's lame practitioners. I have traced a line down, a collapse, a devolution, as snark increasingly loses its intellectual complexity and wit. Now we must dive into ambitious digits and fading newsprint.

Anatomy of a Style

———•———

In which the author names the principles by which snark is carried out in today's usage, distinguishes among its operating methods, and names some of the perpetrators, exposing them to the disapproval of the public.

How does snark work now? Snark is hazing on the page. It prides itself on wit, but it's closer to a leg stuck out in a school corridor that sends some kid flying. It pretends to be all in fun, and anyone who's annoyed by it will be greeted with the retort of "How can you take this seriously? What's wrong with you?"—which has the doubly aggressive effect of putting the victim on the defensive. No one wants to argue with a joke, so this is shrewd as far as it goes. But some of these funsters are mean little toughs. Snark seizes on any vulnerability or weakness it can find—a slip of the tongue, a sentence not quite up-to-date, a bit of flab, an exposed boob, a blotch, a blemish, a wrinkle, an open fly, an open mouth, a closed mouth. It exploits—slyly, teasingly—race and gender prejudice. When there are no vulnerabilities, it makes them up. Snark razzes pomp, but it razzes certain kinds of strength, too—people who are unaffectedly serious. Snarky writers can't bear being out-

David Denby

classed by anyone, and snark becomes the vehicle of their resentment and contempt. It's the sour underside of a liberated media culture, bumper stickers for the electronic age.

Actual comedy is hard work—harder than dying, according to the actor Sir Donald Wolfit, who remarkably announced this truth when lying on his deathbed. But snark, eschewing work, adopts the mere manner of wit, as if manner were enough. How does snark operate these days? Let me count the ways. Snark adheres to one or more of the following practices:

The First Principle of Snark: The "Whatever" Principle. Attack without reason. What, for instance, is the point of this January 2008 post from the popular political-gossip blog Wonkette, which covers goings-on in Washington, D.C.?

CHELSEA CLINTON LEARNS TO SPEAK, LIKE THE HUMANS DO

> Give credit to the Clintons for the job they've done raising Chelsea. Chelsea was born deaf and dumb, a veritable "wild child" who the schoolteachers couldn't tame. But after 20-odd years, through Bill and Hillary's tutelage, she now speaks "words." And since she's young, she can use this new talent to talk to other young people about her struggle with muteness. It wasn't an ordinary job, getting this demon to speak like a person. But Bill and Hillary aren't ordinary people.

It has the form of parody—it conveys to the reader that some kind of earnest claim (that, say, the Clintons brought up Chelsea well) is being put down. The post is failed low snark—obscure rage and sheer ineptitude choke any possibility of laughter. On June 2, 2008, the day of Senator Edward Kennedy's surgery for a brain tumor, Wonkette posted as follows: "Beloved Taxacusetts [sic] senator and last-surviving RFK/JFK brother Ted Kennedy is in the hospital today after doctors fixed a clogged artery in his neck. They successfully removed the Jameson bottle and now he's 'resting.' " This at least makes touch with something—with readers who know that the senator has lifted a glass now and then. But what kind of mind offers this joke on a day in which Kennedy might have died from brain surgery? Ruthless wit directed at the powerful should always be encouraged, and Kennedy's boozing and womanizing are certainly grounds for satire, but wait, at least, until the guy can put his feet on the floor.

Wonkette's insensitivity, like so much of snark, has a proudly idiotic flavor; it seems to be goosing false piety of some sort. You could dismiss it as inane, but the malice of it—the free-floating contempt in a void—gets to you. And the three-dimensional opportunism of it, too. Why not simply ignore it, then? Well, many people do, but the gas of snark enters the air around us as a corrosive sense that cynicism is hip and everyone is vulnerable. Even Michael Phelps's *mother*, for God's sake, gets her picture posted on the Web looking a little funny, with an accompanying gibe. Isn't she fair game? And Shia LaBeouf's mother, too. She has a pair of goggles or something on her head. Go for it. Tom Cruise's two-year-old daughter? Sure, why not? "Tiny mind-controller Suri Cruise decided that she wanted parental units Tom Cruise and Katie Holmes to meet up with Ben Stiller and his wife Christine Taylor for dinner. I'm not sure why Suri was so hell bent on meeting up with them, but I don't question her ways." This text, which appeared on a number of celebrity Web sites in August 2008, accompanied a photograph of Suri carried by her mother as the two couples and their children were fighting their way out of a restaurant. The baby's face was scrunched up, her hands raised high to block out the paparazzi flash pops.

At a higher level, attack-without-reason works by separating distaste from argument. Nothing needs to be demonstrated or argued. Just attack. In a *Vanity Fair* blog, the talented culture and media critic James Wolcott wrote, "A new book by Elizabeth Kendall (*Where She Danced, American Daughter, The Runaway Bride*) is always a welcome event (as opposed to the latest Rorschach pigeon spatter from Joyce Carol Oates, just to pick a name wildly at random)." A Rorschach pigeon spatter? You may not like Oates's writing, but she's a highly conscious artist. I don't see whatever my psyche discovers in Oates's work, I see what she has put there; and whatever Wolcott sees, he feels free to attack "wildly at random." To be the most adept towel snapper in the locker room may not amount to much: Wolcott has been doing this sort of thing, in one place or another, for more than thirty years.

Joe Queenan is another gifted writer who has rolled up decades in the snark trade. Queenan happily proclaims that "I have never deviated from my chosen career as a sneering churl," a remark whose chummy self-approval might cause anyone to envy his untroubled sleep. But then one remembers that Queenan has called Arnold Schwarzenegger stupid, and that he once announced that the blind are lucky because they "get to go through life without ever seeing Shelley Winters," and one begins to wonder if he ever gets anything right. As it happens, the sighted got to go through life seeing the young Shelley Winters, who had love affairs with Marlon Brando, Burt Lancaster, and William Holden, and was married to Italian heartthrob Vittorio Gassman. Winters was a luscious knockout for years. As for the middle-aged woman whose heft so unsettled Queenan, she brilliantly parodied herself as a culture vulture in Stanley Kubrick's

Lolita (1962) and as an indomitable Jewish mother in Paul Ma-zursky's *Next Stop, Greenwich Village* (1976). Queenan has writ-ten about all sorts of things, but one of his specialties, mock movie criticism (*Confessions of a Cineplex Heckler* and other books), is a particularly rich area for snark. There's tons of junk around at any one point, and Queenan has spent years banging around in the sub-basement of movie culture, kicking empty beer cans against the wall, emerging to ridicule hapless pictures that no one ever took seriously in the first place. Fearlessly, he comes right out against Sylvester Stallone; he ruminates fre-quently over the careers of Pia Zadora, Lou Diamond Phillips, and Antonio Banderas. Snark revels in mock celebration of fail-ure. It's living, if you abandon yourself to it.

The Second Principle of Snark: The White Man's Last Stand Principle. Appeal to common, hackneyed prejudices, the more common and hackneyed the better. But disguise the appeal a little, if you can. Race, it turns out, is snark's very heaven. The knowingness that racial snark appeals to is usually concealed backstairs somewhere in the commodious house of un-conscious fear, intolerance, and distrust. Consider the following examples. They are all old news, familiar from the 2008 election season, but listen to the teasing appeal of snark running through them:

> "OUTRAGED LIBERALS: STOP PICKING ON OBAMA'S BABY MAMA!"
> —A CHYRON (HEADLINE) RUNNING DURING
> A DISCUSSION OF MICHELLE OBAMA ON
> FOX NEWS, JUNE 11, 2008

David Denby

"It should be known that in 2008 the world shall
be blessed. They will call him . . . The One."
—THE OPENING WORDS OF A McCAIN AD
ATTACKING BARACK OBAMA

"Even if you never met [Barack Obama], you
know this guy. He's the guy at the country club
with the beautiful date, holding a martini and a
cigarette, that stands against the wall and makes
snide comments about everyone who passes by."
—SPOKEN BY KARL ROVE TO REPUBLICAN
INSIDERS AT A WASHINGTON POLITICAL
CLUB, JUNE 23, 2008

Ah, Fox News. The first example, a clumsy attempt to shove
Michelle Obama into the class of unwed black teen mothers, was
so bizarrely inappropriate that the network quickly withdrew it.
The second example, part of an elaborately facetious McCain attack ad, with Obama surrounded in halos, had two audiences. To
anyone above the Mason-Dixon Line, it seemed nothing more
than a sour reference to Keanu Reeves's savior character in the
Matrix movies. In the South, however, it may have functioned at
another level: "The One," according to Southerners, is a put-
down of someone getting above himself and is likely, in this context, to be taken as derision of an "uppity" black. The third
example, Karl Rove's debonair moment, was *definitely* a coded
put-down of uppity blacks (it turns out that when a black man
gets a college education, he's an "elitist"). At the literal level, it's
nonsense. Obama, whatever his faults, isn't snide, and his beautiful date could only be his wife. Blacks couldn't get into many
country clubs until a few years ago, and not that many are members even now. Surely this was Rove's way of singling out Obama

as the guy with phony Ellington swank who goes where he's not wanted. The most generous interpretation of the remark is that Rove has been snarking for so long that he simply slipped into stupidity, but I doubt it, just as I doubt that Sarah Palin, when making her crack at the 2008 Republican Convention about Obama's experience as a community organizer, was doing anything but arousing people's fears of an organized black mob. These bits of snark appeal to prejudice by coding racism as a joke that, at the conscious level, hides what's being said. The listener's unconscious then does the dirty work, making the connection the snarker wants him to make.

Throughout the presidential campaign, groups of Obama haters attempted, as Nicholas D. Kristof of the *New York Times* put it, to "otherize" Barack Obama by insisting in e-mail campaigns that he was a Muslim, had taken his oath of the office on the Koran, had spent time with terrorists, and had performed many other picturesque un-American activities.* I'm not speaking of the crazies who genuinely thought Obama was the Antichrist, but of conscious political people who spread around joking nonsense because they knew it was likely to be believed by the gullible, the frightened, and the ignorant. Kristof wrote as follows: "What is happening, I think, is this: religious prejudice is becoming a proxy for racial prejudice. In public at least, it's not acceptable to express reservations about a candidate's skin color, so discomfort about race is sublimated into concerns about whether Mr. Obama is sufficiently Christian. . . . Nobody needs to point out that he is black, but there's a persistent effort to exaggerate other differences, to de-Americanize him." Kristof might have added that the attacks on Obama were more virulent than against

* *New York Times,* September 20, 2008.

David Denby

other candidates precisely *because* race was explicitly unmention-
able; the excess was provided by frustration. Snark was the preferred mode of expression in this de-Americanizing project, the
juice that shined up the smear.

Misogyny, at this point in American life, is so lame that you
would think no one would dare pull it out of the trunk of proper-
ties, but it keeps popping up and grinning at the audience. Snark
appeals to a layer of knowingness, as follows:

"The reason [Hillary Clinton's] a U.S. senator,
the reason she's a candidate for president, the
reason she may be a front-runner is her husband
messed around."
—CHRIS MATTHEWS ON MSNBC,
JANUARY 9, 2008

"When [Hillary] reacts the way she reacts to
Obama with just the look, the look toward him,
looking like everyone's first wife standing outside
a probate court, OK?"
—MIKE BARNICLE ON MSNBC,
JANUARY 23, 2008

"As Leon Wieseltier, the literary editor of *The New
Republic,* once told me: '[Hillary's] never going to
get out of our faces. . . . She's like some hellish
housewife who has seen something that she really,
really wants and won't stop nagging you about it
until finally you say, fine, take it, be the damn
president, just leave me alone.'"
—MAUREEN DOWD, IN HER *NEW YORK TIMES*
COLUMN FOR SEPTEMBER 30, 2007

"[Sarah Palin's] primary qualification seems to be
that she hasn't had an abortion."
—CAROL FOWLER, SOUTH CAROLINA
DEMOCRATIC CHAIRWOMAN,
SEPTEMBER 10, 2008

Barnicle is a veteran Boston journalist with plenty of salt in
his talk, and if only he had said "like *my* first wife," his joke, partly
about himself, would have at least sounded the authentic note of
white-guy sourness, like Rodney Dangerfield in a routine from
about 1970. By making it "everyone's first wife," Barnicle, reach-
ing out to men in general as a knowing audience, turned insult
into snark. Like Barnicle, Wieseltier also appealed to the anguished legions of the henpecked. As it happens, Hillary's refusal
to give up her drive for the presidency made her seem more like
a Masada warrior than a housewife. But snark doesn't make its
way in the world by overestimating anyone, as Carol Fowler's
comment on Palin suggests.

**The Third Principle of Snark: The Pawnshop Principle.
Reach into the rotting heap of media referents for old jokes,
old insults, and give them a twist.** Snarking writers try desperately to scrape the rust off a hand buzzer. They long to plump up
a discarded whoopee cushion. Housewife from hell—badda-*bing*!
After Hillary Clinton lost the nomination, Camille Paglia wrote
(on June 11, 2008) in the Internet magazine *Salon* as follows:
"Hillary for veep? Are you mad? What party nominee worth his
salt would chain himself to a traveling circus like the Bill and Hillary Show? If the sulky bearded lady wasn't biting the new president's leg, the oafish carnival barker would be sending in the
clowns to lure all the young ladies into back-of-the-tent sword-
swallowing." The geography of Paglia's circus is a little confusing,

but, getting to the point: One of snark's habits—not quite a principle—is to pretend to be shocked by sexual misbehavior in order to appeal to an audience's supposed distaste for it (the pretense is a mild form of demagoguery). The unorthodox feminist and literary critic Camille Paglia has in fact been a noisy champion of sexual liberties for decades. In a 2005 documentary devoted to the wretched porn movie *Deep Throat,* she said that the movie marked "an epochal moment in the history of modern sexuality." What, then, changed her position on sword swallowing except the desire to commit snark? And is Paglia actually opposed to an aggressive woman who goes after what she wants? Her strenuous metaphors can't hide the fatigue and incoherence of the old taunts.

Liberals are not without sin. In late June, a fund-raising appeal, signed by Democratic operative Paul Begala, went out by e-mail from the Democratic Congressional Campaign Committee. Begala described a Republican fund-raiser in Washington from the previous week: "You should have seen the joint: wall to wall fat-cats. The limos were lined up around the block. If you'd stood in the middle of the ballroom and yelled, 'Hey dirtbag!' a thousand necks would have snapped around." Did Begala really write this kids' stuff? *Dirtbag?* Snark, and right out of the inner quad, where Obama's supporters would have heard freshman-week taunts like "dirtbag." In mid-September 2008, the Obama campaign launched a Spanish-language ad that linked John McCain to Rush Limbaugh. The Limbaugh words quoted in the ad (". . . stupid and unskilled Mexicans") were actually taken out of context and distorted; the linkage relied for its effectiveness on the audience's prior distaste for the snarling Limbaugh, a case of de facto snark. Comparable example from the right: In a hapless article from the *Austin American-Statesman* of July 20, 2008, the writer, Patrick Beach, asserted that Speaker of the House Nancy Pelosi (D-California) was "arguably so left-leaning that her parenthetical should be D-Beijing." China is certainly authoritarian, a nationalist-capitalist hybrid nightmare, but does it make much sense to see it as "left" anymore? Moss is growing on Beach's keyboard.

Are these phrases, and hundreds like them, abominable, the end of civilization? Is the Apocalypse coming soon? Mainly they're examples of terrible writing and thinking, spiked by malice aforethought. But they're bad in a peculiar way. They have a definite tone, and, for a large audience, they scratch a recurring itch. They draw on what might be called *superfluous anger,* which presents itself to the snarker and his fans as entirely justified nastiness. The joke—attempted joke—disguises the bizarre rancor from both parties. By saying this, I don't mean to separate wit from anger. Some of the funniest tirades have been inspired by rage (see Mark Twain on James Fenimore Cooper's "Literary Offenses" or Philip Roth's early novels). But what I've quoted are examples of failed wit. They try to resolve criticism into a phrase, satire into an attitude. At the moment, snark stinks up the air without liberating any laughter.

Since the early nineteenth century, the colloquial ease and play of this country's banter, at its best, has been shrewd and funny in a way unknown anywhere else. During the Depression, the American wisecrack (heard on the radio, in the movies, in newspaper writing) restored a condition of hope and sanity to a population knocked flat on its back. A little bit of the benevolent and sometimes corny folk humorist Will Rogers goes a long way with me, but, in the thirties, the man did say, "We are the first nation in the history of the world to go to the poorhouse in an automobile," and also, "We are the first nation to starve to death in a storehouse that's overfilled with everything we want," two cracks that capture the bewilderment of hard times in the world's richest country and penury in the midst of rampant consumerism. Rogers spoke of "we," by which he meant everyone, or almost everyone. Those two mild jokes are more to the point than ever, but Rogers would seem too tame now—not only because he refuses to attack enemies but because he doesn't use snark. Neither did the universally popular Charles Chaplin, W. C. Fields, and Groucho Marx. Chaplin's Tramp wanted civility and decency in personal relations, only to have the entire world intervene; Groucho and the other Marx Brothers overthrew pomposity and sham while trying to succeed themselves through some piece of shameless trickery; W. C. Fields's was the solitary and selfish individual whose enjoyment of body comforts was disrupted by children, shrews, and idiots. What united these wildly diverse men was a sense of the individual making his way, or failing to make his way, in a hostile society. There was no club of the knowing, but only the great audience. They invited everyone to join in their emotions.

The Depression was a great source of humor as well as woe, with people trading stories of hardship in a raucous spirit of companionship. My own youth, in the fifties, was galvanized in fantasy by the smart-talking broads in thirties movies like Joan Blondell, Ginger Rogers, and Rosalind Russell, and also by the male journalists that appeared in such newspaper comedies as *The Front Page,* in which the reporter was a cynical rowdy at ease in the city, a bottle in his hand, his hat back on his head, talking at a speed that almost defied auditory comprehension. The journalist and the fast-talking working girls were no respecters of reputation. They were perhaps the most obvious example of the popular humor of the period—wised up, cynical perhaps, but not condescending. In the forties, there was the foul-mouthed G.I. and Rosie the Riveter, defiant, wrench in hand. Whatever its miseries, the country in the thirties and forties was at peace with itself spiritually: We were all in the same boat. But at the moment, the attitude is that there *is* no common boat, and that, if there were one, other people should be thrown out of it. Income inequalities and Rovian tactics that exacerbate ethnic and class differences have made for sandpapery relations or blank indifference, and snark serves not to break down the walls of loneliness and fear but to solidify them by servicing communities held together by resentment. This isn't the place for economic and sociological analysis, but everyone knows there's an infinite amount of anger out there. Snark has become the handiest way of repackaging the anger as smear.

Which leads to **The Fourth Principle of Snark: The Throw-Some-Mud Principle. Assume anything negative said about someone with power is true—or at least usable.** The powerful, of course, should be constantly monitored and unmasked, and no one in a democracy expects everything said about them to be fair. "It is an extreme rudeness to tax any man in public with an untruth," Sir Walter Raleigh said. "But all that is rude ought not to be civilized with death." Raleigh, an actual wit, meant that not every slander should lead to a duel. No, and not every insult should be withdrawn or, once given, avenged. We can all toughen up a bit and forbear. But snarking writers regularly ignore even the pretense of truthfulness, and silence in the face of near libel may allow trash, through repetition, to attain the solidity of truth.

When writers of snark turn their attention to anyone even slightly well known, they choose to regard rumor as fact, accusation as proof, gossip as news. Once something negative is said, snark repeats and pumps up the remark, with nasty commentary added as a tweak. Issued from protected territory, snark stands for nothing and lets other people make fools of themselves. Indeed, as far as the readers of snark can tell, just about everyone is a fool; just about every piece of behavior is hapless, or greedy, or pretentious, or just out of it. In a *New York Times Magazine* article, "Exposed" (May 25, 2008), a young blogger named Emily Gould made an account of her working method. In 2006 and 2007, Gould had worked for Gawker, a New York–based media gossip site that glories in snark, and she described her former job as follows:

> *When I started, the site was posting about 40 items per day, and I was responsible for 12 of them. The tone of these posts was smart yet conversational, and often funny in a merciless way. Confronted with endless examples of unfairness, favoritism and just plain stupidity among New York's cultural establishment, the Gawker "voice" was righteously indignant but comically defeated, sighing in unison with an audience that believed nothing was as it seemed and nothing would ever really change. Everyone was fatter or older or worse-skinned than he or she pretended to be. Every man was cheating on his partner; all women were slutty. Writers were plagiarists or talentless hacks or shameless beneficiaries of nepotism. Everyone was a hypocrite. No one was loved. There was no success that couldn't be hollowed out by the revelation of some deep-seated inadequacy.*

These last sentences, presumably, reflect Gawker's working assumptions, not the writer's personal views. But what a set of working assumptions! No one is worth anything; the corrosive view is the only view. Gould says she was "confronted" with "endless examples" of unfairness, favoritism, etc. But how does Gawker know that the accusations it hears are true? Gawker rarely checks its sources. Its writers rarely make follow-up phone calls; they don't search for confirmation elsewhere. Explaining to a prospective Gawker employee what the site does, Nick Denton, the owner of Gawker Media (which controls twelve sites, including Wonkette), wrote that he was "not interested in think pieces unless they're rants." Denton went on: "The ideal Gawker item is something triggered by a quote at a party, or an incident, or a story somewhere else and serves to expose hypocrisy, or turn conventional wisdom on its head, and it's 100 words long, 200 max." There's snark's mission statement—indolent parasitism as a work ethos. And there's snark's Strunk and White style guide, in 50 words max.

This is the way snark journalism works now: The writers for Gawker or other gossip sites hear some accusation from a tipster or a sorehead, or read it in a newspaper, and then, after spicing the salad with dropwort, lay it out on the table, where it will remain forever (the Internet does not clear away its dirty dishes). But has it never occurred to these writers that people with power even the smallest amount of power—are bound to have enemies? That anyone slighted or passed over might be using Gawker and other Web sites or publications to settle scores? Twenty years ago, *Spy* magazine, at its worst, made itself available to New York media people for this purpose: Items would turn up claiming that some midlevel editor sweated too much or didn't wash his hands after using the john, or committed some other atrocity that only a coworker could have known about (or would fabricate).

Snarking writers want to appear wised up about everything, but, in their eagerness to be of service to the malevolent or jealous, they can be stunningly naive. On April 25, 2005, Alessandra Stanley, the TV critic of the *New York Times,* wrote of Katie Couric that "lately her image has grown downright scary: America's girl next door has morphed into the mercurial diva down the hall. At the first sound of her peremptory voice and clickety stiletto heels, people dart behind doors and douse the lights." Are we reviewing office reputations now? If three people don't like you for any reason, you could get a bad "image"—especially if a journalist is ruthless enough to report it. A famous broadcast journalist like Katie Couric can take care of herself, of course. She'll use those stiletto heels. But what's wrong with stiletto heels, anyway? As I noted about that Paglia quote above, snark has its priggish tones, its semidemagogic habit of pretending to be shocked in order to appeal to the presumed distaste of a large audience. This is a common hypocrisy at the sites owned by Nick Denton— peeking through disapproving fingers at the allegedly outrageous behavior of everyone in town, and then giving the posts a little twist of snark in order to make disapproval sound hip.

One way of looking at a Web site like Gawker is that it's partly a parochial phenomenon. Like the editors of *Spy,* many of its writers come from outside New York, but, once they hit the city, despite their journalistic ambitions, they become the latest version of Manhattan party kids clamoring for a little attention— and getting it, in this case, by posting on the site or setting up their own blogs, attacking people, getting attacked in turn, and generating, if not buzz, then at least a hum of irritation and envy, a few limo rides, some clothes, a good time. The pathos of their situation, as Vanessa Grigoriadis explained it in a brilliant *New York* magazine piece ("Everybody Sucks," October 15, 2007), is that the Gawker writers who joyously celebrate the troubles of the established media can't make enough money to live decently in New York. As Grigoriadis put it, "Youthful anxiety and generational angst about having been completely cheated out of ownership of Manhattan, and only sporadically gaining it in Brooklyn and Queens, has fostered a bloodlust for the heads of the douchebags who stole the city. It's that old story of haves and have-nots, rewritten once again." Hence the bitter sarcasm directed at the mainstream. Gawker's snark is one of those cases of outsiders banging on the gates. *Let me in, you worthless, undeserving bastards!* In fact, as soon as jobs open up in the same established publications that the young writers have been attacking, they take the jobs. As they move up in the magazine, newspaper, and cable TV world, they take their prose with them, and readers and viewers get a journalistic culture of snark.

But let's go beyond New York provincialism. This habit of snarking your enemies could move into Web sites devoted to any kind of public event—a business conference, say, or a town council meeting. You give a speech at a PTA meeting, and someone takes your picture, or notices a small error or a maladroit remark, or just doesn't like something you said, and he posts your picture on a community Web site with anonymous nasty commentary. Paranoid? It's already happening. We know about Big Brother— the federal government listening in on phone conversations as it hunts for terrorists—but it's Little Brother, the neighbor with the iPhone, who may be the scariest monitor in the future. I don't believe, as culture critic Lee Siegel insists in his hand-wringing 2008 tract, *Against the Machine: Being Human in the Age of the Electronic Mob,** that the Internet is stealing our souls. But

* Spiegel & Grau, 2008.

I'm not crazy about it stealing my likeness on a routine occasion and assigning someone else's meaning to it. Digital technology makes such monitoring easily possible. On campus, students may snark their professors (as well as each other—see the Fifth Fit). Small communities post photographs of undesirables with prison records or men who make derogatory remarks to women on the street. Do we really want cybercops everywhere, snarking away at neighbors? Some of the cops may be properly enforcing community norms, like school crossing guards, but others could be just malicious busybodies and snoops, gleefully mucking up other people's lives in a righteous spirit. Snark covering itself in morality is uniquely nauseating.

In the digital age, the old notion that your personal *honor* was bound up in your reputation may no longer be a sustainable idea. There's nasty stuff floating around about many of us; virtually no one's reputation is unsullied, and trying to control all of what is said is obviously impossible. As Raleigh insisted, you needn't defend your honor on every occasion, and now you *can't*. In the future, one definition of character may be the ability to choose which insults to take seriously and which to ignore. As a preliminary general rule, I offer this obvious advice: Don't respond to anything unless it interferes with your ability to make a living or lead a happy social life.

The Fifth Principle of Snark: The Reckless Disregard Principle. Ignore the routine responsibilities of journalism. The more flagrantly you ignore them the better. In the Internet age, the rumor, the smear, or the taunt, if it's pungently phrased, spreads instantly through the Web; and from thence into the mainstream press. The Internet will quickly turn snark into meme. And once the item appears, its truth or falsity is irrele-

vant. The phrase, the insult, has an existence in the media (someone *said* it, didn't he?), so it can be referred to, combined with other items, revived, denounced, dismissed as old news, and so on. The false item, made memorable by snark, passes through the entire cycle of media life. This is known as "the national conversation."

Why take back anything that might get *at* someone? Both journalistic irresponsibility and the appeal to backstairs prejudice come into play in the rumor that there was a videotape in which Michelle Obama used the term *whitey*. The rumor was mentioned again and again on cable news in the spring of 2008, even though no such tape showed up. The denials issued by the Obama campaign themselves made a story, so *whitey* got mentioned yet again. This is journalism practiced along snarkist lines. Earlier in the campaign, there was a funny example of the never-take-back-a-snarking-item method. I choose this example because it's harmless, even charming in its way, so one can study the process without anger. First, the writer Rebecca Traister, in the Internet magazine *Salon,* published a piece in November 2007 about Michelle Obama. Second, a commenter, decorating the story anonymously from behind a handle, insisted that he had read the uncut transcript of the interview with Michelle, and that it had contained remarks about the Obamas' sex life that Traister had left out of her article. The alleged remarks were a testament to Obama's youthful virility in the morning. "Morning wood" was the relevant phrase.

Whoopee! Time to get moving! The Web site Jezebel sprang into action. It posted a cover of the magazine *VIBE* with Obama looking at his watch ("It's Obama Time") and decorated the illustration with snarky commentary: "Ever wonder what it was like to wake up next to America's chain-smoking, coke-sniffing trillion-dollar tax increase advocating biracial Indonesia-reared predicted winner of the Iowa caucus?" The sex-in-the-morning story certainly didn't make Obama look bad, though it crashed in on his privacy like a bulldozer knocking down a wood-frame house. Rebecca Traister, however, insisted that the anonymous commenter had never read the transcript, which, in any case, contained no secrets of the Obama bed, and the prankster confirmed this to Jezebel. In other words, the entire thing was hooey. Jezebel admitted as much, but kept the item and its commentary intact.

The habit of never checking the truth of anything—a habit that exists at sites more serious than Jezebel—wrings bitter tears from the angels of journalism. Web sites and blogs go back and forth between saying, "We're *not* journalism, we don't have the time and resources to check things," and saying, "We're doing a better job than mainstream journalism in ferreting out the truth."* It can't really be both, I think. If you're going to fling a handful of firecrackers at people from behind a bush, you probably shouldn't, at the same time, demand praise for your aim. Snark and the Internet are co-enablers. The Internet satisfies snark's need for instant circulation; snark satisfies the Internet's need for attention-getting semilibel. What if the anonymous prankster had said that the Obamas slept with a loaded revolver between them? If you're never going to check anything, why not post it?

The Sixth Principle of Snark: The Hobbyhorse Principle. Reduce all human complexity to caricature. Then repeat the caricature. In the past, as in Juvenal's bizarre testament to Mes-

---

* The excellent political site Talking Points Memo makes a continuing effort to check what it posts.

salina, snark has at times been complex, even ambivalent. At the moment, in its degenerate phase, snark is always simpleminded. By definition ad hominem, it nevertheless has little interest in what anyone actually *is*. Genuine seriousness, when it turns up (say, in a man like Al Gore), disgusts snarky writers—they refashion it into stiffness, pretension. The mystery of personality bores them into silence.

Snark "reads" people on sight often by reducing them to a trait, a label, a moniker denoting failure; then, in a sly (and sometimes funny) tautological process, it may institutionalize the caricature it has itself created. Celeb sites find an epithet for someone—"homewrecker Sienna Miller"—and then repeat it, until it becomes a meme. *Private Eye* referred for years to the English (now American-based) editor Harold Evans as "small but perfectly formed." No one unacquainted with Evans had any idea what this meant, but the mere repetition of it was funny. The hope of American snarkers, in imitation of *Private Eye,* is that persistence in using epithets will turn a joke into a kind of cult. *Spy* had an obsession with short men that was initially funny precisely because it was meaningless. "Back in the good old days, Runts were discreet, deferential. The New Short, however, have dispensed with such social mores and can be seen shamelessly flaunting their puniness in public." Okay, this is not bad as a spoof of the clichés of trend journalism, though one has to point out that, in 1977, a good decade before *Spy*'s article, Randy Newman had *already* satirized prejudice against the short—and by implication against any group—in his hit song "Short People" ("They got little noses / And tiny little teeth / They wear platform shoes / On their nasty little feet"). But the magazine kept at it; the editors really had a thing about short men. They made lists of fallen short celebrities, short billionaires, short editors at the

Condé Nast media company, sometimes accompanied by photos of them with their taller wives. They tried hard to build a mock prejudice, but, a few years later, when it was clear that a cult of insulting the short had not developed, this bit of snark just seemed bizarre, and it fell away. Today, it would become a meme; shortness would prevail as an insult.

The Seventh Principle of Snark: The You-Suck Principle. Glom on to celebrities in an attitude of adoration and loathing; first adoration, then loathing. The celebrity culture in this country has now engulfed politics, sports, business; it has engulfed culture. Kids grow up in it, taking it for a natural environment, and even to speak of it seems odd, since naming it implies some distance from it or control over it. But distance or control are impossible, since virtually everyone, including me, lives in it, breathes it, is fascinated and disgusted by it. Just the same as everyone else, Ph.D. students immersed in Hegel or the intricacies of early Victorian landscape painting sit around leafing through celebrity magazines—"He's hot . . . she's *so* hot." I would not make myself a prig by writing about celebrity if I did not share some of its obsessions. In any case, snark is central to its workings.

Consider the typical cycle: A young actor, actress, singer, rapper, model, athlete, or writer is built up rapidly, and receives our adoration, even awe, and becomes the object of a million fantasies of companionship, lust, and possession. Everyone wants to be with the fresh stars, talk to them, sleep with them. The new talent, in the beginning, eagerly yields herself to the process. Nothing is more pleasurable than the attention of strangers. Young performers love the excitement of it, and they fall into the hands of managers and publicists who tell them a little scandal won't hurt. You need to get out there, to establish your brand. Athletes seek endorsements; actors and actresses want bigger roles and better up-front money; rock singers wants bigger tours; and writers, moldy from years of indoor work, need air and some way of selling a few books. The publicists tip off the paparazzi, who snap the celebrity's picture as she steps out of a limo, and the tingle on the back of her neck is like the first taste of champagne.

The young stud, the starlet, the athlete—they are all in play. Magazines like *US Weekly,* the infantile celebrity blogger Perez Hilton, and literally dozens of other celebrity sites fawn all over them. *Vanity Fair,* in one of its recurring fantasies of great Hollywood stars (Gretchen Mol? Orlando Bloom? Natalie Portman? Jessica Biel?), puts them on the cover in pale, luminescent nakedness or drapes them across five other young things, posed in evening clothes against a white background. Immortal stars! Just like Bogart and Ava Gardner! In Los Angeles and New York, desperate invitations arrive: Please, *please* appear at openings, celebrations, charity events. They are paid serious money—thirty, forty thousand dollars—to go to parties for an hour, often in clothes that are given to them. Strangers take their picture on cell phone cameras and sell them to Web sites for a few dollars. Their tattoos are a source of wonder. They are easily seen naked or at least shirtless on the Internet.

At that point, the smartest fresh celebs, feeling that tingling sensation turn into a sting, take it as a warning sign: *Withdraw a little. It's time to make myself boring.* Who knows if the desire to have many, many children is not partly an attempt to throw off the paparazzi? Certainly the desire to sell pictures of one's children to the media (and then donate the money to charity) is an attempt to go around the paps. It's a power move, of course: *Even snaps of my tiny offspring are worth a lot of money.* In any case, the attempt fails; the tots are pursued, too, and then arrayed in groups on the cover of magazines ("Hollywood's Cutest Kids"), six of them at a time, in a kind of celebrity-infant bake-off. You don't have to be Swift to see that we are eating our children.

The celeb is hooked; he may even have special chummy relationships with certain photographers or magazines, letting them know when he's going out. Or he's trapped; the gossip industry closes in on him. Publicists not only tip off Web sites or magazines about the whereabouts of the star in return for favors, they feed their media contacts squalid rumors about rival celebrities who are represented by rival publicists. The star, bathed in gossip and cynicism, now lives his life along snarkist lines. Who knows what happens to these people internally? A few, like Matt Damon, marry outside the movie colony, and keep their lives hidden. As for the others, it's a good guess that if the star hasn't already made himself a grotesque, the attention turns him into one. Despite pious protestations that he wants privacy, he may be addicted to adulation. Anyway, the paps, and the amateurs, too, pursue him on the street, at a bar, outside a restaurant, at the Los Angeles airport. Sometimes the pursuit turns vengeful. An actor or actress a few pounds out of shape is a scandal, an outrage. Blurry photographs of an actress at dinner, or holding a baby in a doorway, turn up in the media, and she looks awful in most of them, partly because she doesn't want to be snapped—she's wearing shades and a hood, her hand is up, she's snarling at the photographer.

Hollywood has been a magnet for the most beautiful young people in the country for ninety years, and we have always been looking at them. What's new is that digital media and the Internet have brought us much, much closer. The public no longer relies, as it did generations ago, on a few gossip columnists to feed them information and an occasional picture in a newspaper or a fan magazine. The celeb Web sites never let up, and the public is not gazing in worshipful passivity, it's taking pictures and sending them to the sites, and then commenting with crazy relish on the pictures and the posts surrounding them. Everyone plays; professional blogger and amateur stalker have joined together, and they provide information for the rest of us, who own the celebrities' bodies, opinions, and love affairs. All of that belongs to us.

The tone of the comments is coarse, invasive, obsessional. On the Internet, no one is under any compulsion to obey the postal laws. For instance, Perez Hilton, the celebrity blogger who gets millions of hits a week, scrawls obscenities on the pictures of his victims ("FIST" on a picture of a closeted gay star) and adds dribbling whitish liquids from their mouths, a case of snark illustration. His writing, running below photographs, is just a few lines of undernourished gossip. Hilton, who was born Mario Armando Lavandeira, in Miami, evokes a kind of snarko-magical version of high school, with manufactured celebrities replacing hall-locker rivals. A throwback to an old-fashioned gossip columnist from 1935, this Internet phenomenon exercises his power whenever he can. His essential message is, "Baby, you're *mine*." A snapshot of a couple on a beach is accompanied by the following: "**Ashley Tisdale** and her on-again boyfriend, boybander **Jared Murillo,** hit up the beaches of Hawaii on Thursday. The Tiz and her man didn't seem too pleased to find the paparazzi eagerly snapping away at them. Oh well, if you don't like it, then don't go to Hawaii if you're famous!" Basically, don't go anywhere.

If a given star slips and falls—has a few flops, a bad season, a drug episode, a poorly received book, a few casual sexual escapades with the wrong person (which may be no more than what a young, good-looking office worker would get away with)—snark swings into action. Adoration is followed by a quick withdrawal of affection and fake expressions of moral disapproval. A magazine that has been publishing pictures of a handsome young actor wearing almost nothing is suddenly shocked to discover that he easily picks up girls on a movie set, on a vacation, at a party. And disapproval is followed in turn, perhaps, by an abrupt shove into the gutter. Suddenly gossip mags and Web sites are invested in the star's failure; they want her ground down into nothing. It's a deathwatch. The press and public can't get enough of her atrocities. The god or goddess, hit by a stone, bleeds, and therefore has to be killed as a betrayer of faith. They are no longer divine, and we will prove it by murdering them. Drug-dazed screwups like Britney Spears or Amy Winehouse are pursued until they collapse or throw a punch. An actress or singer may be addressed on the Web as "bitch"; her legs, breasts, and skin are examined for flaws; she's then criticized for being snippy toward a celebrity press which, in fact, is doing everything it can to kill her. Actors, singers, and athletes are pulled out of closets, often by gay fans, or accused of cheating on their girlfriends or wives. Athletes are caught with the wrong women, or just with women. The Web pursuit of them turns furious, obscene. (Barry Bonds is loathed, Alex Rodriguez is snarked—his greatness and obvious vulnerability to criticism bring out the Crazy Ants of the Web.) Movie directors who had a few early hits followed by a flop are suddenly discovered to be "pricks"—arrogant losers doomed to struggle and get nowhere.

In the feverish cycles of obsession, snark functions as the avant-garde of resentment. The best put-down lines are pure snark, which sets and extends the tone of derision. In August

2008, the *New York Times* ran a page in the Sunday Style section with pictures of aging actresses who have erased their wrinkles with Botox. Fair game, I would say, since Botox makes women look weird, though the movie critic in me would also point out that fifty-nine-year-old women who aren't named Streep can't get starring roles in Hollywood. Botox and other forms of "work" are a desperate career move to stay in the game. Anyway, the accompanying text to the *Times* piece consists of speculation that the offending celebrities have gone soft in the head. It seems a Botox ingredient—botulinum type A—may have drifted from their skins to "one hemisphere of the brain." In brief, Botox is making them stupid. That Botox has been around for a long time and has caused no evident outbreaks of stupidity among its users is brushed aside. Snark is in play.

The actresses' real problem, of course, is that they got older. Tom Cruise is also getting older, and that Cruise is a "creep" is now the common impression of the American people. Maybe he *is* a creep—what do *I* know? He has certainly made an ass of himself, scolding Brooke Shields for taking antidepressants to fight postpartum depression. But Cruise, like him or not, is in a difficult place in his career. A moderately talented, hardworking actor, he's gone a long way on hustle, and he has now entered the uncertain terrain of early middle age. Maybe he'll become a more interesting actor, maybe he'll fade away. Who knows? But it's his sudden vulnerability in early middle age, as well as his religio-pharmaceutical views, that make him a dream target. The Hollywood Gossip: "The heat that Tom Cruise emitted early in his career has long evaporated, leaving only a smirking corpse in its wake. Cruise struts around like a smaller, yappy version of Arnold Schwarzenegger as *The Terminator*," etc. It's all gloat and jeer in a mounting rapture of justified hate.

But enough! To hell with the celebrities, what about us? Initially, we grant that someone is prettier or more talented than we are. The act of giving over part of our self-love and strength to another should be natural, easy, joyous, but it isn't for many. In the common estimation, American life is a viciously competitive race, in which every ego has to fight for a limited amount of oxygen. In that atmosphere, then, adoration of another is experienced as a loss, a wound. Reduced in some way, we want to hit back. For instance, the snarky sports site With Leather has the following words as its logo: "With Leather is a blog about all the assholes and idiots in the world of sports, and the hot chicks who date them." Let's assume that the logo is partly a self-mocking joke (*we admit we're voyeuristic creeps tracking athletes' sex lives*), but, still, the mix of adoration, envy, and resentment in that one sentence is startling. When the athlete slips, the resentful part of the mix takes over. Why not *me*? Why do *you* get to be famous? Why do *you* get laid? Admiration flips into hatred, and the ego is repaired, restored, and soothed in snarly put-downs. The snarky sports sites (Deadspin is another) not only exult in the messes athletes get themselves into, they also make fun of the career choices of failed athletes, who, apparently, have to be clobbered even *after* they drop out of the NFL. The punishment for capturing our love never ends.

But there's no point in going on. We're trapped in this forever. Almost everyone participates in the narrative of ascendancy and decline. The national ritual may lead to recurrent bouts of nausea, but a sick stomach never stopped anyone from consuming for very long. Not just celebrities, but any man or woman who does public work, or performs, or wants fame, enters the realm of snark and gives himself over to a public, large or small, that keeps a kind of stock-market quote in its heads marking the exact value of every player at any given moment. Snark helps set the price, particularly for the short sellers.

There's a poignant footnote to the celebrity cycle—sites like Hot or Not, in which anyone can post a snapshot of himself or herself and ask for a rating on looks. Posed uncomfortably in a doorway somewhere, her back arched against the frame, a girl in jeans vamps for the camera; some shirtless guy with a few muscles stands on the balcony of his San Diego condo or sits atop a picnic table chugging beer. Eager for attention, they want a touch of fame on the Net, and maybe some action to follow. Hot or Not has evolved into a dating site—people who approve of each other's appearance link up. Well, when digits give way to flesh, good luck to them. But by offering themselves up to be judged, the participants are buying into the snark culture. They're brave or foolish enough to risk contact with the clawed beast of snark, daring themselves to see how long they can stay in the cage with it. *Here I am, judge me. Will I be destroyed by what you say?*

There are other principles so obvious that they hardly need illustration. For instance, **The Eighth Principle of Snark: The Pacemaker Principle. Attack the old. Your editors and Web publishers want young demographics, so they won't mind.** Snark is about punishment. The ambitious, the overweening, the allegedly pretentious, anyone who does anything, anyone who merely exists; they all have to be punished. But the spectacle of age goes beyond mere existence. Age is infuriating, disgusting: the looming winter, the failing body, the terminating scythe. Snark functions as ill humor applied to a universal condition, and the knowing group includes all of us. Which means we might lose whatever good things the old might give us—perspective, depth, gravity, all things anathema to snark. The old—and not just the ones running for president, who deserve it—get their slowness clocked, their verbal flummoxes written down, their sags and humps measured. In the *New York Times,* on February 17, 2008, Charles McGrath wrote, "Jim Lehrer, 73, has been with 'NewsHour' since 1975, so long that some of his early viewers are now in assisted living." Ka-*ching.* Or perhaps, ka-*flooey.* The sentence has the setup of a good one-liner, but snark pours a drop of poison into the ear of wit, and the punch line dies on its feet. A few months later, television critic Ginia Bellafante noted in the same paper that "A cameo [in the soap opera *All My Children*] by [Warren] Buffett, the 77-year-old chairman of Berkshire Hathaway, is probably not the obvious path to a younger audience and advertisers for products that have nothing to do with incontinence." No, perhaps not the obvious path—thanks for the tip. Then there are the fashion magazines that post, on their Web sites, amateur pictures of the sagging, blotched, and mottled flesh of ordinary middle-aged people walking on some forlorn boardwalk. The sites then give commenters free rein to publish their disgust. A sixtyish couple in which the woman is gaining weight and the man wears a bulging thong excites a particularly exuberant contempt. Is there no tenderness for the sexual vanities of proud, aging bedroom champions?

The Ninth Principle of Snark: The Gastronomic Principle. Attack expensive, underperforming restaurants. There's at least one case, I think, in which punishment is deserved, and barbarous snark sounds just about right. Eater.com brings news of New York restaurant openings, chefs moving from one kitchen to another, and the like. The site also offers restaurant reviews, sometimes culled from other sites, but it's not a rating service, like the invaluable Zagat. To an outsider, the site comes off as a gathering place for vengeful hangers-on in New York's competitive restaurant world. When a pretentious restaurant—big space, fancy decor, ambitious menu—opens up, Eater swings into full, snarky glory. Most of the prose about such places is ribald, disgusted sarcasm, and things can get a little rough. The contributors, for instance, engage in solemn discussion of whether a certain enormous bad restaurant should be called a "shitshow." Still, one can be entertained by the rough justice of the invective. Who hasn't been robbed by one of these places or by a comparable version in another city?

> *The restaurant's signature dessert is a Baked Alaska that comes shaped as a beehive, accompanied by a bee made of stale white chocolate and Cheerios.* Cheerios. *You've seen this dessert before, at FAO Schwarz. At Kobe, it's $18 and is listed on the menu in a ridiculous* featured dessert *box.*

Eater offers the eternal rancorous voice of the diner whose pocket has been picked. There isn't much this disgraced and dangerous creature can't complain about—too little service, too much service, the drabness of the clientele, the absence of clientele. When a restaurant is in trouble, Eater launches the tumbrel to the scaffold. The site has an amiable feature called "Deathwatch," in which, at periodic intervals, correspondents gaze upon a failing restaurant's empty tables, its desperate attempts to change the menu or decor. "Deathwatch" is pure sadism, the bitter underside of consumerism—snark's dream of a fat victim that has been felled by its own excesses. Snark pecks away until the agonizing death is achieved. But isn't it justified in this single case? I am moved by a wave of tenderness: Vicious snark is necessary when it amounts to protest against oppression by overpriced dining.

When I began this little book, I promised myself I would not merely ask everyone to be nice, and I don't think I have. But, obviously, some sort of positive ideal is animating the many dislikes, high and low, serious and trivial, that I've given air to—if not an ideal like Matthew Arnold's demand for "sweetness and light," which has a noble but faint and tinkling sound to us, like exquisite music heard from far away, then at least a notion of judgment formed by adult experience. The snarkers sound like kids—and not like wild, beautiful, and crazy kids, either, but like hoods and brats. Since many of them are not kids but adults, we can point out to them that they are not punching their weight, that they are settling for too little in their own writing while ignoring the damage they are doing to conversation and to themselves (imagine a life in which a snarking attitude toward everything is enough!). I am not calling for a puritanism of language but, on the contrary, for a paganism of language in which every sensuous apprehension of the surfaces of life is filtered through a developed sense of how the surfaces and the interiors fit together, and what matters and what doesn't. This notion of judgment, or what I called *grace* at the beginning of the book, is vague, I realize, but perhaps it will become clearer as we go on.

In an earlier period, we thought that in the free market of ideas and language, the best and most truthful expression would win out and the rest would be forgotten. Now, I'm not so sure. During the 2008 election, Barack Obama was subjected to an enormous amount of innuendo, slander, and coded racist insult ("Muslim," "terrorist," etc.), but, at the same time, myriad defenders in the press and on the Internet unmasked or refuted the snark directed at the beloved young Democratic Prince. One could say that the enormously expanded communication system attained a kind of equilibrium, in which every powerful untruth was countered by an equally powerful truth. But in this case only! What about everyone else? They will not be defended.

I have a tendency, I know, to be bothered by cynicism, slander, and failed, nasty wit more than I should, and, indeed, to take things too seriously in general, yet I think the genuinely bad stuff should be noted. There is, after all, no inherent reason why a democratic media society has to be stupid. In the past, the snickers of a few journalists have killed lousy practices or stupid phrases in public conversation. It would be awful—a real defeat—if we had become too jaded or overwhelmed in the expanded media environment to do nothing about similar things now but shrug them off as inevitable.

The Conscience of a Snarker

———◆———

*In which the practice of anonymity reveals its dark side, the
shift from media irony to media snark is analyzed, and the
practice of knowingness is deplored.*

Faceless

A comedian performs in front of an audience, and the
possibility of silence, boredom, or resentment opens
before her like a pit widening at her feet. In thirty
minutes of stand-up, she tries to walk a tightrope across the pit
to the safety of audience adoration.* And then, good night or
bad, she goes out the day after and faces a new audience, risk-
ing failure all over again. Indeed, failure is possible in any kind
of public performance—a lecture, a speech, a talk before a
business group or at a town council meeting. But snark, produced from the safety of a bedroom or a newspaper or magazine

---

* As Steve Martin put it in *Born Standing Up* (Scribner, 2007), "The comedian's slang for a successful show is 'I murdered them,' which I'm sure came
about because you finally realize that the audience is capable of murdering
you."

column, faces only one kind of rejection: that no one will notice it.

Snark is like a schoolyard taunt without the schoolyard. It wants to get into your face without presenting a face of its own. In an actual schoolyard, a forward drives for the basket and a guard harasses him, tries to force him into a mistake, and the guy with the ball works his elbows to throw off the defense while trash-talking all the time. The two men work each other hard. The insults lock together, grow louder and funnier, but all within the structure of a game. Trash talk may be derived from African oral traditions, but it's also a spiritual descendant of "heroic invective"—the insults exchanged between warriors before combat in the *Iliad*. The Greeks and Trojans would meet on the field, threaten, bluster, tear down one another's country and lineage, and then fight to the death. Part of their manly valor consisted of words. In trash talk, no one dies, but the valor of words remains. It's much the same thing with doing the Dozens: Two men, or two women, standing right on top of each other, let loose a tremendous patter of insult, each topping the other until victory or exhaustion. Trash talk and doing the Dozens are stirring and funny, obviously, because both people are *there:* Ego is attached to presence within a social formality that gives the encounter meaning. The street and the basketball court are still communities in which public opinion arbitrates reputation— communities governed by honor and shame, like the aristocratic courtyards in which dueling was a way of settling a quarrel.

Practiced that way, insult is an art; sometimes, it even explicitly assumes the form of art. Scottish poets in the sixteenth century abused each other in a public exchange of scornful verses—"flyting," it was called. The poet William Dunbar says to Walter Kennedy:

Snark

Yit mycht thay be sa bald in thair bakbytting,
To gar me ryme and rais the feynd with flytting,
And throw all cuntreis and kinrikis thame proclame.

To which Kennedy, properly outraged, and quickly altering the name of his foe, responds:

Dirtin Dumbar, quhome on blawis thow thy boist?
Pretendand the to wryte sic skaldit skrowis?
Ramowd rebald, thow fall doun att the roist,
My laureat lettres at the and I lowis;
Mandrag, mymmerkin, maid maister bot in mows, etc.

Pretty rough stuff, if you ask me, and it goes downhill from there. American cowboys in the nineteenth century had cussing contests in which the winner got a new saddle (and maybe a few drinks and a trip upstairs to a soft bed, too). It was a face-to-face contest, and someone with an exquisite sense of filth had to judge the results.

But snark plays no game in which one might win or lose. People who start their own blogs almost always identify themselves, but many snarking writers exercise power anonymously, hiding behind a handle, attacking people who appear in public, who run blogs, or other commenters. The insult comes out of nowhere, as if waiting for an occasion. But why hide? This love of anonymity is amazing to me. If you have something to say, why in the world would you want to hide yourself? I know that, years ago, opinion columns in some magazines, as well as the book reviews in English literary weeklies and "Talk of the Town" pieces in the *New Yorker*, were unsigned, but, in hindsight, the practice looks coy—a misguided attempt to speak with an institutional voice about something that should have been personal. Newspaper editorials remain unsigned because they *are* the voice of the institution. But a comment is always personal, and no one's handing out grades: If everyone has the right to speak in a new medium, why hide behind a handle?

The answer, of course, is that the anonymous writers are either ashamed of what they're saying, or, alternately, quite proud of what they're saying, but, in either case, they're not eager to confront anyone directly. In the Internet, we can louse up the world. Anonymity frees us to attack whites, blacks, Muslims, men, women, gays, birders, arachnophobes, philatelists—frees us in a way that would be impossible in the office, at a cocktail party, in a bar, or in a schoolyard. Anonymity allows us to air the nuttiest or angriest part of ourselves, the wild fantasist inside the mumbling student, the ornery political protester inside the working mother, the slap-happy adolescent inside the medieval scholar. Or perhaps, putting it more generously, the anonymous bloggers and commenters want to escape into an alternative life, a made-up identity; they want to launch a doppelgänger into the Net, a version of themselves that is opinionated, swaggering, profane, wild, and free. Or perhaps bold, trenchant, and serious. Or completely frivolous. In the end, whether mean or sweet, crazy or sane, the alternate identity, handled rather than named, can always be cut loose, just like the astronaut in *2001* whose lifeline gets snipped, stranding him in endless space. You don't have to take responsibility for an alternate identity. If anyone comes close to you, you can kill the Internet double. But the insults stick around and could possibly do damage in some future era; the space garbage can always be retrieved by the faithful probe Google.

Anonymity is a strategy with a long history, good and bad, but I dislike it as a hiding place for snark. This uneasiness makes young people, and especially teenagers, go blank. In my experience, they don't attach any moral valence to anonymity at all. When grown-ups say to them, "Say whatever you want, but stand behind your words," they don't see what the fuss is about. Anonymity, for them, is part of what makes the Internet a delight. It's a medium you don't have to *pay* for—so much of it is free, without cost, including the cost of responsibility.

This difference in attitude may be a new version of the generation gap: For anyone over fifty, the idea of anonymous communication comes attached with a powerful charge, sometimes negative, sometimes positive. Kafka's *The Trial,* finished in 1925, begins as follows: "Someone must have slandered Josef K., for one morning, without having done anything truly wrong, he was arrested." That line echoes throughout the twentieth century as a portent of the anonymous denunciations that were a regular practice in the totalitarian era. Yes, a phone call to the secret police is a much more serious act than a snarking post, but that's the kind of negative vibe anonymity can give off—it's not something to be played with; it has dangers lurking in its secrecy. The good vibes are all associated with liberation. Dissidents or human-rights advocates who publish or send e-mails in repressive regimes rely on anonymity as a protection against prison, exile, and death. Without anonymity, they can't freely exchange ideas and information. Protest may begin in anonymity. The historian Robert Darnton, in his various books on the literary underground of prerevolutionary France, has chronicled the role played by scurrilous anonymous pamphlets in discrediting the ancien régime. Anonymity protected the firebrands, and now it protects the workers at American corporations or government agencies who want to complain about official policies without getting fired. Anonymity is a tool for whistle-blowers of all sorts.

Anonymity is never a neutral position, and if the anonymous using the Internet are not a little smarter, they could mess themselves up, or mess other people up. If students anonymously spread snarky opinion or gossip around on a campus Web site, or on a social-networking site, yes, the social atmosphere becomes electric with tensions and sexual innuendo, hurt feelings mixing with the desire to be loved, or at least appreciated, and this can be exciting. Anonymous snark (as well as praise, of course; but snark has higher entertainment value) is part of the erotic ambience of school and campus life. But that's putting it as pleasantly as possible. On a popular national Web site like Juicy Campus, what begins as snark quickly rots into abuse. Most of the posts have the jeer and bluster of a bad frat-house party. Each campus is identified on the site, and the question "Who are the hottest girls on campus?" quickly gives way to "Who are the biggest sluts?" The women are named, but the men identifying them hide behind a handle.

How much is anyone hurt by anonymous Web insults? For people well established in whatever it is they want to do, Web insults have a curious insubstantiality; they exist in an ontological haze. If someone slams you at a party, or at work, you can talk back or take a swing at him. If someone libels you in the *Los Angeles Times,* you can call your lawyer. The attack is direct, present, and either serious or not. But an attack on the Web feels wispy; it's literally ethereal, like some gas in the room that you cannot smell. People you know may read it, but it's also possible that they will never even hear about it. Even if you have good reason to feel paranoid, you can choose not to notice what's been said. You could avoid Googling the blogs for references to yourself, or avoid community message boards, and so on. Surely, if we all get snarked now and then, we should also be tough enough to shrug

Snark

it off. Anyway, it may be an advantage to know that someone detests you. An early warning of opposition, a jolt to self-esteem, a notice that there may be a hostile world out there—none of this should put you off your game for very long.

But for kids, who often live or die by what others think of them, it's a different story. If you're a student sitting quietly in a classroom, taking notes or drawing flowers on a doodle pad, or chewing on the end of a plastic pen, there's a fair chance that some kid sitting nearby thinks you're a *whore* or a *dickhead,* or perhaps a *douchebag,* or possibly, phrasing it with greater intricacy, a *fetus-faced douchebag.* That person wants you to jump in a lake and get drowned, and may say words to that effect on the Web. Cyber-bullying is a serious problem in some high schools, leading to depression, or, in a few cases, suicide. (In Japan, the government is contemplating stepping in and doing something about it.) As for insults on Juicy Campus and the other trashy campus sites, I would love to take the good-guy, libertarian position and say that reputation smashing and shaming (complaining about someone's bad behavior) are regrettable but essentially harmless—an inevitable part of the healthy roughhouse of a free medium. But I don't believe that shaming is harmless, and I doubt that the professional good guys—the law professors who are fighting to keep the Internet open—know how much anonymous slagging of individuals goes down on the Net. On Juicy Campus, the pathetic old sex pathologies, cloaked by anonymity, all come bursting out, free and proud. A guy sleeps with a girl, and then punishes her for going to bed with him. ("That girl [name of student] is the nastiest most pathetic whore on the face of the earth. She's had four different nose jobs and she's STILL looking beat!" and much more. No body part or organ goes untouched.) A post like that may be ridiculous, but it appears all the

David Denby

time, and anonymity protects the bounder. (What she thinks of *him* is never recorded.) When the comments are not directed at women, they are directed at gay students still in the closet. ("Does anyone else know this tool gay faggot freshman who thinks he's tough shit for being in college. Wears wife beaters and has poofy nipples. This kid is trying to compensate for the fact that he's gay, just listen to how he talks. He pops Adderall like Flintstone vitamins and he cannot keep his mouth shut," etc.). This is snark with a righteous leer, as if the writer thought he had some profound civic duty to expose gay men. Since he's anonymous, his friends will never ask him why he finds the entire subject so interesting.

Young men have always dumped on women, and men who are uneasy about their own sexuality have always bullied gays, but anonymity has created neo-cads who are running rampant. And these guys could bully people into sexual retreat on campus. Even if the person attacked doesn't care all that much about reputation, and even if the other students reading the posts know that they are garbage and laugh them off, this sort of thing may have an intimidating effect, and the damage, in another way, can stretch into the future. Suppose a woman was sexually adventurous in college, or a man did a little cocaine as a sophomore. How many of us *didn't* screw around in this way? An employer looking to make a hire ten years later is going to Google that job candidate, and the assertion—true or not—lodged in a social-networking site or Juicy Campus will leap off the screen. If you're a law partner making the choice, or a human-resources interviewer, are you going to take the chance that the hire could blow up in your face? It's safer to Google a fresh candidate. Something the "whore" and "stoner" did at nineteen—or something someone *asserted* they did—could tear a hole in their lives years after the fact.

All these issues have been raised most persuasively by Daniel J. Solove, a professor at George Washington Law School, in his 2007 book, *The Future of Reputation.** Solove's point is that reputation may not have much of a future. For two hundred years or more, he says, America was a country in which you could move around, wipe out your past, and get a fresh start somewhere. You carried your reputation with you, or you discarded it and built a new one. In the future, however, you may not have that freedom—not if a dossier of your follies trails around after you like a finger-pointing ghost. I would add that snark guides the finger to the place where it can do the most damage. These posts appear in the first place because someone wants to be funny and nasty. No one goes on a campus site to report on another student's sexual or drug behavior in a spirit of solemn disapproval. Snark provides the tone, the form, the lure. The reward for being catty—some sort of response on the site from commenters—makes snark more likely to happen. But what the snarking gossip doesn't realize is that his freedom to express himself could take away someone else's freedom down the road.

Some of these arguments, however, may not register with kids, for the simple reason that privacy doesn't mean to them what it means to their elders. Millions of kids may disdain anonymity and be perfectly willing to sign posts—and sign a lot more than that. They *want* their secrets out there. The notion of an interior space where you can act without observation or judgment, where you can harbor mysteries, fantasies, hopes, make terrible remarks, bury your mistakes, behave well or badly, but, in any case, do it in solitude or only with a lover or friend—that's a situation that is losing its prestige in the digital age. Privacy doesn't much register

* Yale University Press.

as a spiritual value and a sanctified space anymore. Yes, I'm aware that, for many kids, Facebook allows them to create an innocuous persona out of their tastes and interests, like the inside of a locker covered with stickers. No harm there, but many older kids are giving up their secrets, too, or perhaps, on a blog, offering a running account of their love life, the progress of an affair, both heartbreak and triumph. In that case, they are offering themselves up to be snarked—in effect, joining the snark culture, because the comments that show up after they expose themselves are not going to be nice. Commenters want to entertain, they want to be clever, they want to burn, they want to snark your dying grandmother and your broken heart. Why offer yourself up to them?

Media Irony Becomes Snark

In 1999, at the time of the sex-in-the-Oval-Office rumpus, a young man named Jedediah Purdy wrote a very solemn tract called *For Common Things.** The book was an attempt to reject the cynical, derisive national mood of the late nineties. Purdy's enemy was irony—not the sharpened blade used by Swift and generations of satirists, but something much less strong. Purdy meant a style of self-presentation that was defensive, weak-backed, even self-deprecating—a style, said Purdy, generated by living in the media, in which no human emotion, no sentiment came without its mocking pre-echo from some movie or TV show:

> *Irony is powered by a suspicion that everything is derivative. It generates a way of passing judgment—or placing bets—on what*

* Random House, 1999.

kinds of hopes the world will support. Jerry Seinfeld's stance resists disappointment or failure by refusing to identify strongly with any project, relationship, or aspiration. An ironic attitude to politics and public life never invites disappointment by a movement's decline or a leader's philandering. There is a kind of security here, but it is the negative security of perpetual suspicion.

If you didn't believe in anything in the first place, your hopes couldn't be dashed—you couldn't be hurt by failure. For Purdy, this mood was a kind of national disaster. A healthy political and civic culture was impossible without a minimum of trust and belief.

At the age of twenty-four, Jedediah Purdy was an exceptionally earnest fellow, and I'm not sure I would want to live in a society reordered according to his ideals. For one thing, he was rather pious about the cows, the ditches, and the thunderstorms of his rural upbringing in West Virginia, where the people making maple syrup were apparently far more consequential than the wicked sophisticates in the big cities. Were there any jokes on the family farm? Or corrupt pleasures like an occasional visit to a movie theater? The glumly virtuous young Purdy could have used a little ironizing himself. Still, he articulated, with some eloquence, his uneasiness in a culture that refused to take anything straight, and his book hit a nerve.

In recent years, our culture has gotten better and worse. Whatever else the rise of Barack Obama means, it certainly suggests that the kind of college-educated young people Purdy was talking about have become eager to reject shallow cynicism and to embrace hope in the public sphere—and, more to the point, to take power and change the tone of public discourse. In this same period, what Jedediah Purdy meant by irony has split into two directions: In political commentary, it has climbed into something tough and cleansing in the comedy of Stephen Colbert, who repeats, in exaggerated form, the jeering, wrapped-in-the-flag manner of a reactionary pseudomoralist like Bill O'Reilly. In Colbert's comedy, ironic exaggeration is the strong arm of satire. Another part of Purdy's notion of irony—the fear of being taken in by anything—has collapsed into snark.

Purdy assumed that ironists had beliefs they wanted to protect: "We do not want the things in which we trust to be debunked, belittled, torn down . . . So we keep our best hopes safe in the dark of our own unexpressed sentiments and half-forbidden thoughts." Snark is the further media degeneration of this attitude, a manner in which there are no remaining "unexpressed sentiments and half-forbidden thoughts," no romantic self that needs safety and protection. What would engage a romantic self? Art, for one thing. But contemporary snark is postaesthetic. It's produced by people living in the media who know, by the time they are twelve, the mechanics of hype, spin, and big money. Everything that isn't part of the entertainment business cycle seems lifeless and unreal to them. Compare them to an earlier generation: When the hard-nosed journalists of an earlier era played at verbal takedowns, they were assuming the role of streetwise, ink-stained wretches, clawing their way ahead in a tough game. But today's college-educated models all know they are participating in something called "the media," and their awareness of the profile their attacks give them—and of the role their work plays in the media ecosystem—reinforces their snarkish tendencies.

How did we get to such a sour situation? Consider the special case of book reviewing. In March 2003, in the first issue of the magazine *The Believer,* which is sponsored by Dave Eggers's publishing house, McSweeney's—very much an antisnark outfit—

the critic and novelist Heidi Julavits wrote a good-humored but pained attack on snark in book reviewing. Julavits, like many literary people in recent years, bemoaned the reduced prestige of literature in America, a situation she blamed on both the rise in the universities of "cultural studies" (in which students may study sitcoms, Madonna, and parking lots, but not literature) and the power of television to smack audiences across the face with "the real" in ways that literature, for many people, can't easily match. In this curdled atmosphere of low prestige, a critic's snarky put-down of an ambitious book is a way of attracting attention and, perhaps, as literary critic Sven Birkerts has suggested, of relieving the critic's anguish that he no longer matters very much.*

Julavits found it hard to separate justified cruelty in criticism from mere critical showing off. (I agree: One can't make general rules about it; one can only go on a case-by-case basis. As the critic Clive James has written, criticism is a performance that judges someone else's performance, and some snark is inevitable.) Julavits gave an example of justified cruelty—the occasional nasty piece by literary critic James Wood,† a writer who has an almost religious belief in great writing. When Wood is disappointed, he can turn vituperative. "Faith," Julavits said, "is intrinsic to his intellect. His disenchantment is part and parcel of his elation."

Elation, of course, is precisely the emotion—engaged, passionate, jubilant—that is anathema to writers of snark. Their jaded negativity attacks any kind of aspirational tone that doesn't

---

* "Critical Condition," *Bookforum,* Spring 2004.
† Wood's literary essays can be found in the collections *The Broken Estate* (1999) and *The Irresponsible Self* (2004).

conform to a commercialized notion of hip. Even when something original and great comes along, snarking writers cannot turn off their attitude for a minute and celebrate. In the end, they wind up serving as thugs of the media conglomerates, breaking the arms of anything out-of-date or unsalable or truly idiosyncratic.

Apart from outright nastiness, the commonest form of snark in arts criticism at the moment is false knowingness. Some critics, especially young ones, affect an omniscient manner: Media-saturated, they have heard everything, seen everything, read everything, and they assume an air of ineffable sophistication and weary familiarity. "From time to time, residents of England produce advancements in that nation's major art forms: narcissism, glibness and camp," Choire Sicha wrote in the *New York Times,* on March 9, 2008. Yes, a true foe of glibness. Sicha, a former writer for Gawker, has a talent for this kind of high-twit nonsense. On May 13, 2008, in the weekly *New York Observer,* Sicha launched one haughty non sequitur after another in an attack on young male American writers. "The American desire for fucking has become, locally, the Brooklyn-based or -bound desire for a book deal and a brownstone. Men, finding that they cannot really get status or security from the ownership of women very often, find their very selves disparaged. Like most of us, they get their status first from consumption, and the way out is to become a maker of consumables; a high-class published author." Gibberish like this gets written when publications are willing to substitute attitude for the kind of plain English sentence that gives facetiousness little room to hide. As it happens, many young writers, artists, actors, dancers, and theater people in general live in Brooklyn because, among other reasons, Brooklyn is beautiful and Manhattan is unaffordable. Perhaps a Brooklyn sensibility in the arts will emerge in a few years, something as distinctive as the mutinous and playful tone of Greenwich Village in the 1920s. Why snark it in its cradle?

Scratch a writer of snark, and you find a media-age conformist and an aesthetic nonentity. Recognizing no standard but celebrity, indifferent to originality or to quality, snark may be out-of-date or fading almost as soon as it's filed (or posted). The media are always moving, like time itself, and snark becomes time's fool—it has to scramble to keep up. Perhaps that's one reason why writers of snark seem so bitter: They know they are cutting the path of their own extinction.

Maureen Dowd

————•••————

Wherein the most talented writer of snark in the country is
called to account for her malevolence and naïveté.

————•••————

In the spring of 2008, I was sitting in a coffee shop on Broadway, on Manhattan's Upper West Side, and a tall, straight, fine-looking woman, about eighty-five years old, mysteriously stopped at my table. We were complete strangers. She was holding a copy of the *New York Times* in her hand.

"Did you read that woman today?" she said. "I think she's mad." And then she walked out, without another word.

————•••————

Maureen Dowd, the popular Washington columnist of the *Times,* can make other political writers look obtuse and bland. She assumes certain things that give her an enormous advantage—rhetorically, at least. She assumes that everyone in politics is out for himself; that principles or beliefs in a politician are a set of self-flattering delusions; that the powerful are moved by jealousy, rivalry, narcissism, and fear of every sort—fear of being thought weak, most of all. She knows everything about poseurs and posing. But does she know anything else about politics? Utterly repelled by piety and righteousness, she also seems bored by genuine advocacy. Disgusted by unbounded ambition, she never seems to wonder what an ambitious leader might *do* besides gratify himself.

Her appetite for ridicule equals any politician's appetite for power, and maybe the two hungers aren't all that different. On the page, she attempts to dominate the mighty, exacting the revenge of the weak. Of course, political writers have often done that. If they aren't insiders, what else can they do? Yet there's something oddly naive and puritanical about Dowd. How, one wonders, does a politician define himself, attract others, and assume leadership without some degree of calculation, conscious self-dramatization, and even mythmaking—exactly what Dowd sees as ridiculous? In all, it is lucky for her that she didn't get to describe Lincoln on his way up the ladder; she would certainly have shredded his county-lawyer, Honest Abe racket. And Franklin Roosevelt! A vain patrician tooling around Hyde Park and dreaming of voters in workmen's caps. He might promise work to the poor in order to get their votes, but men of his class can't see past the end of their cigarette holders. Yes, she would certainly have had them both down cold.

More than anyone, Maureen Dowd has been funny about scandal and disaster. She has scored again and again, and no one—including, I suspect, the old woman in the coffee shop— wants Dowd to beat her swords into knitting needles. Gentleness is not the antidote to snark. Comedy can be as savage as a serpent's tooth if it's accompanied by a few good ideas, and that's where the problem begins. Maureen Dowd has rhythm, pace, timing, an extraordinary ear, an amazing memory for odd bits of cultural flotsam. She's a brilliant aphorist who, in a few words, can say something it would take another writer paragraphs to spell out. She uses all the traditional tools of comedy—exaggeration, lampoon, insult, outrageous puns, fantasia—and gives them her own twist. Born in 1952, in Washington, D.C., the daughter of a police inspector, she was taught by nuns—well taught, it turns out. (She can write a campaign column in piglet Latin: "Obama demonatus est tamquam Musulmanus-Manchurianus candidatus—civis 'collo-cerviciliarus' ad rallium Floridianam Palinae exhabet mascum Obamae ut Luciferis," etc.) She seems to have read everything, and she's shrewd about popular culture, particularly about the way movies colonize the country's unconscious. Yet she has not—as far as I can tell—a single political idea in her head. Not one. Not a policy she wants to advocate or defend, a direction she thinks the government and the country should be heading toward. What is the purpose of politics and government, anyway? She writes as if personality, appearance, and attitude were the only things that mattered. For her, politics is a stupid, despair-inducing entertainment, a tale told by an idiot signifying vanity. Despite all her larks and inventions, she's essentially sour and without hope. In brief, she's the most gifted writer of snark in the country.

During a presidential campaign, she tugs at everyone who climbs into the saddle and sooner or later pulls them off the horse. That Al Gore was a serious man who presented himself awkwardly to the public was no more than a delicious opportunity for her. In the 2000 campaign, she never actually *saw* Al Gore. What she saw, in the classic manner of snark, was the caricature she could make of him. Of course, she razzed Bush, too. She rejected both as dreadful pols—one a pompous prig, the other an ignorant fake populist. She dealt with them as two men whom no woman in her right mind would ever go out with. The sex-and-the-city banter is a terrific comic strategy; it gives Dowd an attractive persona to inhabit—naughty girl looking for a good time—and it brings the men down from their pedestal to the common conceit of combing over a bald spot, sucking in a gut, trying to sound impressive. At the end, when the disputed election fell into the hands of dueling lawyers, in November and December, Dowd mocked Al Gore's persistent desire to win the presidency. Gore, it seems, was a sneak and an egomaniac who covered his ambition with neat grooming and sanctimonious words. This is how she wrote about him on December 10, 2000, before he conceded:

> *You know and I know that if Eddie Haskell ever does have to give that Farewell . . . and Hello Again! address sacrificing a presidency he is sure he won and setting himself up for another run no one wants him to make, it is going to be the most self-righteous, self-aggrandizing, self-serving speech in the history of politics and literature.*

But the concession speech that Al Gore gave on December 13, 2000, was patriotic and entirely selfless. He spoke of past disputed elections and the Constitution, of the need for continuity and national reconciliation. He disagreed with the Supreme Court decision that gave the presidency to Bush, but said that he accepted it and that everyone—and particularly his own supporters—needed to unite behind the new president. That was it. End of speech. No self-righteousness or self-aggrandizement. Now, Gore lost the election because he failed to carry his home state, Tennessee; because Ralph Nader took votes away from him; because the Florida balloting was a mess; and because the Supreme Court made the wrong decision. Yet Dowd and the people who, imitating her, judged Al Gore by the pathetic caricature they turned him into—they also played a part in the outcome.

Al Gore's defeat was snark's greatest victory and snark's greatest disaster.

After a while, Dowd knew. She *knew*. She is too smart not to know. A few months into Bush's term, she apologized—in a way. From April 1, 2001:

> *Forgive me, Al Gore. I used to think you were striving too geekily to be Millennial Man. The PalmPilot on your belt. The BlackBerry. The Earth-cam you dreamed of. Citing* Futurama *as your favorite show. The obsessions about global warming and the information highway. Boldly choosing the first Jewish running mate. But now I'm going hungry for a shred of modernity. Bush II has reeled backward so fast, economically, environmentally, globally, culturally, it's redolent of Dorothy clicking her way from the shimmering spires of Oz to a depressed black-and-white Kansas.*

Yes, fine; wonderful last sentence. But all of Bush's traits were apparent at the time she was stuffing Gore's shirt. And even in the act of apologizing, she had to turn Gore into a scarecrow all over again.

In the next few years, Dowd took apart the Bush administration. She hated its anti-intellectual bent, its turning "moral values" into a club wielded against anyone with different ideas. As the country staggered into disaster, she grew more and more contemptuous. She treated the president ("W.") as a boy, and she sloshed beer all over him at the barbecue pit: "When W.'s history is written, he will be seen as the rebellious teenager crashing the family station wagon into his father's three most cherished spots—diplomacy, intelligence and the Gulf." After the presentation of the Iraq Study Group's report in December 2006, which advocated staged withdrawal, she wrote: "Poppy Bush and James Baker gave Sonny the presidency to play with and he broke it. So now they're taking it back." But she was mistaken; they couldn't take it back. The president may have appeared, in Dowd's Freudian family drama, as a petulant child trying to outdo his father, but he was in fact a far more stubborn and cunning man than she gave him credit for. As the Bush administration went on, the insufficiencies of snark became mortifyingly obvious. Did it ever occur to Dowd that her chummy, high-schoolish, I-can-see-your-undies routine might be bizarrely beside the point? Given the enormity of the war in Iraq, and the lies used to sustain it—which she exposed as vigorously as anyone—did she ever wonder whether puns and sarcasm were adequate to the task? In the end, the Bush administration embarrassed Dowd's powers of ridicule. Not that Bush was anything like Hitler, but Dowd was very much like Ernst Lubitsch (director of *To Be or Not to Be*) or Charles Chaplin (in *The Great Dictator*) and other people around 1940 who thought that laughing at a tyrant might be the way to humble him. Catching the president in contradictions and hypocrisies, bouncing Ping-Pong balls off the square forehead of "Rummy," or teasing the lugubrious Cheney as "Vice" and "baby-sitter"—none of this came close to an adequate critique of power. Dowd's ridicule didn't help us keep our sanity in hard times, as the movie and radio wisecracks did during the Depression; they contributed to the impotent nihilism of the period. Dangerous lies and irresponsible snark were part of the same despairing mood. No journalist could have changed the course of the Bush administration, but Dowd's scattershots, funny as some of them were, never even amounted to a coherent narrative of what was going on (for that, *Times* readers turned to Sunday columnist Frank Rich, who has a gift for seeing patterns in disparate events).

When something terrible is happening, the feebleness of snark makes you long for an attack that is sustained and sustaining.

The emergence of Hillary Clinton as a presidential candidate put Dowd back in her comfort zone. Here were the embarrassing and exploitable possibilities of gender and sex roles, all in play at once. In January, in New Hampshire, Hillary momentarily broke into tears:

> *There was a poignancy about the moment, seeing Hillary crack with exhaustion from decades of yearning to be the principal rather than the plus-one. But there was a whiff of Nixonian self-pity about her choking up. What was moving her so deeply was her recognition that the country was failing to grasp how much it needs her. In a weirdly narcissistic way, she was crying for us. But it was grimly typical of her that what finally made her break down was the prospect of losing.*

One can find insinuations like this dazzling in their quick procession yet also wonder if any of them are true. Maybe no such calculations and regrets took place; maybe Clinton was just exhausted and lost control for a few seconds. In any case, why was Dowd pretending to be angered that someone who had long sought the presidency might have been upset by the thought of losing it? What's surprising about that? The girlish, kittenish side of Dowd, which has often soothed men even as it teased their inadequacies, was offended by a tigress who used her claws to burst out of her cage. At times, Dowd seemed eager to punish Hillary for her ambitions, as if deep down she were alarmed by the idea of a woman making so great a claim for herself, and snark filled the space where sympathy—or perhaps rueful appreciation—should have been. And, of course, what Clinton actually wanted to *do* as president—which, after all, might have validated her presumption—was of no interest to Dowd. Policy is for drips.

Dowd went back into her damned-if-you-do-damned-if-you-don't mode. She scored off Hillary for her momentary self-pity (if that's what it was) and then for opportunism and ruthlessness. Hillary was a sobbing weak sister dependent on her husband; Hillary was a ball-breaker. Snark exults in the tropes of gender, and Dowd genderizes everything, sexualizes everything. The lactating/buffing contradiction about Gore mentioned in the First Fit pushed him into not one but *two* cartooned states of gender definition. If Hillary Clinton is essentially masculine, Barack Obama is essentially feminine, a man in touch "with his inner chick." After years of mocking the macho posturing of the Bush administration, Dowd was suddenly back in the bar with the boys, teasing a woman who wanted power and a man trying to handle tough competition with grace. Barack Obama was "Obambi"; he was "a pretty boy" and a "diffident debutante." In June 2008, she wrote, "Barry has been trying to shake off Hillary and pivot for quite a long time now, but she has managed to keep her teeth in his ankle and raise serious doubts about his potency." Hillary, she said, was trying to "emasculate" Obama. It's futile to complain that Dowd is heartless, because her humor is produced by heartlessness. But there's something both grasping and pathetic in her dissatisfaction, and she passes that dissatisfaction on to the reader as a kind of blight. The laughter dies before it hits the belly.

The 2008 Democratic party nominating process was, after all, a strange and fascinating struggle: A male candidate couldn't uninhibitedly attack the first serious woman candidate without appearing sexist, and a white candidate couldn't uninhibitedly attack an African American without seeming racist. Everyone was walking on eggshells, though a few condescending remarks broke through the hesitancies and prohibitions on both sides. But this kind of delicate and awkward situation is something that snark, with its reduction of everything to caricature, can't address. Dowd recast a rough but not especially vicious nomination battle into an imaginary sex war; she tabloidized something that was actually far more interesting. Her writing was a desperate, disjointed, and demoralized performance, and it left many readers enraged.

Let us propose the simplest possible ambiguity—that Hillary Clinton hungrily wants power and, with equal desire, wants to alleviate poverty and help people get medical coverage. Isn't it likely that both drives fully coexist within her, rather than, as Dowd would have it, ambition simply runs roughshod over everything else? Hillary got away from Dowd; the journalist never pulled together a coherent portrait of a woman who had obsessed her for years. Before the Democratic convention, in late August, Dowd concocted a fantasia in which Hillary and John McCain were colluding in an attempt to destroy Obama. When both Hillary and Bill Clinton performed well at the convention, selling Obama as best as they could, Dowd never acknowledged the performance, never admitted her misjudgment. Again, she came off as naive: In the end, Bill and Hillary Clinton were not quite the self-absorbed narcissists that Dowd made them out to be but professional politicians, doing their best to sustain their currency in the Democratic Party. And as Hillary was slipping away from her, Dowd found it harder and harder to get a handle on Obama. At one point, she wrote a column in which she complained that Obama's ascendancy meant the country was in danger of losing

David Denby

its sense of humor—as if Dowd's inability to solve her compositional problems were a national issue that everyone should be concerned about.

Like the ravenous Cyclops, snark sees with one eye. And then it complains that other people lack dimensions.

THE SEVENTH FIT

What Is Not Snark

-----◆-----

In which the author gives some examples of nasty,
vituperative, and funny writing that avoid the
weakness of snark.

I s *Countdown with Keith Olbermann,* MSNBC's nightly news-
and-commentary show, a flagrant case of snark? I realize the
entire civilized world is awaiting judgment on this issue.
Olbermann certainly yanks the rug. He imitates Bill O'Reilly's
orotund tones, and regularly includes him in a feature called
"Worst Person in the World" as a kind of Old Faithful of stupidity. Olbermann's use of O'Reilly as an assumed villain works as
snark for his large club of viewers. And the rest of the show? Like
Zeus gathering the winds amid mighty peaks, he marshals political attack with image, joke, and rhetoric, and then lets loose in
whooshing blasts of ridicule. One can't help noticing, however,
that Olbermann's tirades are voluminously factual, astoundingly
syntactical—the man could give excited lessons in sentence
structure to eighth graders—and always logically organized. He
points out contradictions, misstatements, idiocies; he threatens,
mugs, and blusters, and, when he's done, he balls up his script,

David Denby

as if it were no more than an inadequate first draft (letting us know there's always more of this to come), and flings it at the camera, breaking the glass of the TV screen and hitting the viewer in the face: *You sticks, you stones, you worse-than-senseless things! Wake up!* He's intelligent as hell, and no one could accuse him of a common tendency of snark—disengagement from the matter at hand. No, he's obviously a passionate and committed fellow, well informed, with a ferocious memory (or a good staff). So, yes, he may use snark as a weapon, but snark is not his general mode. I would call his show satirical political commentary. So that's settled: Everyone can breathe normally again.

But now a small but rich bouquet of flowers, a few cases of vituperative work that is free of snark. These are the ideals I have been straining for:

On March 4, 1921, Warren Gamaliel Harding, the twenty-ninth president of the United States, delivered his inaugural address to the nation. Three days later, in a *Baltimore Sun* article titled "Gamalielese," H. L. Mencken proposed to analyze Harding's use of English. Mencken, it turns out, was stunned by such sentences as "I know that Congress and the administration will favor every wise government policy to aid the resumption and encourage continued progress" ("the resumption of what?" Mencken asked). And he was stopped cold by the extraordinary "I would like the government to do all it can to mitigate, then, in understanding, in mutuality of interest, in concern for the common good, our tasks will be solved." Mencken summed up as follows:

> Setting aside a college professor or two and half a dozen dipso-maniacal newspaper reporters, [Harding] *takes the first place in my Valhalla of literati. That is to say, he writes the worst*

*English that I have ever encountered. It reminds me of a string
of wet sponges; it reminds me of tattered washing on the line;
it reminds me of stale bean-soup, of college yells, of dogs bark-
ing idiotically through endless nights. It is so bad that a sort of
grandeur creeps into it. It drags itself out of the dark abysm (I
was about to write abscess!) of pish, and crawls insanely up the
topmost pinnacle of posh.*

And so on, for many paragraphs more. Now, H. L. Mencken
can be hard to take. A believer in the Nietzchean superman, he
was always pining for some aristocratic American equivalent in
the form of a revolutionary-era Anglo-Saxon landowner. He was
disgusted by a modern America cheapened by "Italians weed-
grown on exhausted soil . . . Jews too incompetent to swindle
even the barbarous peasants of Russia, Poland and Roumania."
The anti-immigrant Mencken who constantly lampooned democratic man as the great American boob ("He is more ignorant of
elementary anatomy and physiology than the Egyptian quacks of
4000 B.C. . . . . He is as ignorant of sonnets and the Gothic style as
he is of ecclesiastical politics in Abyssinia")—this Mencken, rant-
ing, disagreeable, even a little silly, is mostly unreadable today.
But when Mencken sets himself a specific task, like describing a
political convention or characterizing "Gamalielese," he remains
as funny as Mark Twain. The passage above is vituperation, but
it is not snark. Mencken creates a series of fresh images; he
doesn't resort to some dreary level of reference exhaustingly familiar to the reader.

And neither does film critic Pauline Kael, in her attack on the
British actor Nicol Williamson*:

---

* *The New Yorker,* January 17, 1970.

Nicol Williamson is a violently self-conscious actor whose ef-
fect on the camera is like that of the singers who used to shatter
crystal. And he had the bad fortune to enter movies just when
the new, strenuous forms of sexual freedom were coming in, so
he's gone through more gyrations in a year and a half than
most actors do in a long career. He has already run a gamut of
sexual positions, plus such assorted Jacobean exertions as
drooling, vomiting, murder, and suicide. He goes from being
gracelessly virile to being repulsively masochistic, and, which-
ever it is, he's too much. His wracked and tortured energy
seems to be irresistible to the English directors he works with;
as if in awe of his force, they stand back and let him rage and
snivel and curse. They don't often get an actor with a powerful
animal presence, and they probably hope that Williamson's
thumping virility will keep their movies from being dull, but
[as Hamlet] he just flails around like a self-flagellating wind-
mill. . . . His acting is all pathos and vituperation, snarls and
tantrums. Yet he isn't really strong; he's such a weeper. Bearded,
and with a nasal twang, he's deliberately, wretchedly unat-
tractive. He stares so much he's in danger of wearing out his
eyeballs.

Kael is not particularly trying to be funny here. Apart from "a
self-flagellating windmill" and the parting crack about eyeballs,
there's nothing you could call consciously clever. She's merely
describing her impressions, which, given the nature of Williamson's excesses, turn out to be funny; and she's stating that his
kind of flamboyance is all wrong for movies. It's criticism, blessed
criticism; it's not snark.

One could find many more examples of people writing funny,
angry, personal attacks and writing well. Let's not forget Stephen

Colbert, in his famous appearance at the White House Correspondents' Dinner on April 29, 2006, with President Bush and the First Lady in attendance. Properly dressed in a tux, Colbert did his usual blustering-patriot routine. He spoke as a man who felt close to the president, an admirer, a supporter—no, a brother in arms:

> *Now, I know there are some polls out there saying this man has a 32% approval rating. But guys like us, we don't pay attention to the polls. We know that polls are just a collection of statistics that reflect what people are thinking in "reality." And reality has a well-known liberal bias. . . . I stand by this man. I stand by this man because he stands for things. Not only for things, he stands on things. Things like aircraft carriers and rubble and recently flooded city squares. And that sends a strong message: that no matter what happens to America, she will always rebound—with the most powerfully staged photo ops in the world.*

There wasn't much laughter in the room. The reception was closer to a pained silence. Colbert's jokes were not the usual convivial roast of the president's linguistic misfortunes but an actual critique of Bush's lies, and many journalists felt that he went too far. In the Establishment view of things, Colbert displayed poor taste, and the mainstream press hardly reported his performance. Yet his twenty-minute routine became famous on the Internet, and was eventually taken up by print journalists. I don't think the jokes are Colbert's best, yet the event is still a classic of comedy and of citizenly virtue. Why? Because it's not snark. It's irony, an apparent act of kinship with the president that is actually a violent unseating of the president. Also, it's courageous—Colbert spoke the words to the president's face and suffered the freezing disapproval of the audience. The club members invited Colbert in—made him, like an Athenian, a member of the drinking party—but he turned the tables on them, upbraiding not only the president but the journalists' chumminess with the president. The comic was serious, the journalists were not. Colbert expelled snark from the room.

Vituperation that is insulting, nasty, but, well, *clean,* may live forever. Go and commit some. You'll feel better. You'll make other people feel better.

Reference List

Alterman, Eric. "Out of Print." *New Yorker,* March 31, 2008.

Andersen, Kurt, Graydon Carter, and George Kalogerakis. *Spy: The Funny Years.* New York: Miramax, 2006.

Arena, Valentina. "Roman Oratorical Invective," in the Dominik and Hall anthology listed below.

Bangs, Lester. *Psychotic Reactions and Carburetor Dung.* Edited by Greil Marcus. New York: Knopf, 1987.

Birkerts, Sven. "Critical Condition." *Bookforum,* Spring 2004.

Blumenkranz, Carla. "On Gawker.Com." *n + 1,* Winter 2008.

Boxer, Sarah. "Blogs." *New York Review of Books* 55, no. 2, February 14, 2008.

Craig, Christopher. "Audience Expectations, Inventive, and Proof." In *Cicero the Advocate,* edited by Jonathan G. F. Powell and Jeremy Paterson. Oxford: Oxford University Press, 2004.

Denby, David. "The Contender." *New Yorker,* January 24 and 31, 2005.

Dominik, William, and Jon Hall, editors. *A Companion to Roman Rhetoric.* Oxford: Blackwell, 2007.

Dowd, Maureen. *Bushworld: Enter at Your Own Risk.* New York: Berkeley, 2004.

Egendorf, Laura K., editor. *Satire.* San Diego: Greenhaven Press, 2002.

Gardner, Martin. *The Annotated Snark.* New York: Bramhall House, 1962.

Gore, Al. *The Assault on Reason.* New York: Penguin, 2007.

Reference List

Gould, Emily. "Exposed." *New York Times*, May 25, 2008.

Grigoriadis, Vanessa. "Everybody Sucks." *New York*, October 15, 2007.

Hitchens, Christopher. *The Missionary Position: Mother Teresa in Theory and Practice*. London: Verso, 1995.

Ivins, Molly. *Molly Ivins Can't Say That, Can She?* New York: Vintage, 1992.

Johnson, Samuel. *The Lives of the Poets*. London: Oxford University Press, 1964.

Julavits, Heidi. "Rejoice! Believe! Be Strong and Read Hard!" *The Believer*, March 2003.

Juvenal. *The Sixteen Satires*, third edition. Translated by Peter Green. London: Penguin, 1998.

Kael, Pauline. *Deeper Into Movies*. Boston: Little, Brown, 1973.

Kingsmill, Hugh, editor. *An Anthology of Invective and Abuse*. New York: Dial, 1929.

Kinsley, James, editor. *William Dunbar, Poems*. Oxford: Oxford University Press, 1958.

Kinsley, Michael. *Please Don't Remain Calm: Provocations and Commentaries*. New York: Norton, 2008.

Knight, Charles A. *The Literature of Satire*. Cambridge: Cambridge University Press, 2004.

Mack, Maynard. *Alexander Pope: A Life*. New York: Norton, 1985.

Mencken, H. L. *On Politics: A Carnival of Buncombe*. Edited by Malcolm Moos. New York: Vintage, 1960.

————. *Prejudices: A Selection*. Edited by James T. Farrell. New York: Vintage, 1958.

Morton, Brian. "The Banker's Red Suspenders." *Dissent*, Fall 1987.

Neu, Jerome. *Sticks and Stones: The Philosophy of Insults*. Oxford: Oxford University Press, 2007.

Okrent, Daniel. *Public Editor #1*. New York: PublicAffairs, 2006.

Palfrey, John and Urs Gasser. *Born Digital: Understanding the First Generation of Digital Natives*. New York: Basic Books, 2008.

Pope, Alexander. *The Poems of Alexander Pope*. Edited by John Butt. New Haven: Yale University Press, 1963.

Reference List

Purdy, Jedediah. *For Common Things: Irony, Trust, and Commitment in America Today.* New York: Vintage, 2000.

Queenan, Joe. *Confessions of a Cineplex Heckler: Celluloid Tirades and Escapades.* New York: Hyperion, 2000.

———. *If You're Talking to Me, Your Career Must Be in Trouble.* New York: Hyperion, 1994.

———. *The Malcontents.* Philadelphia: Running Press, 2002.

Seabrook, John. *Deeper: My Two-Year Odyssey in Cyberspace.* New York: Simon & Schuster, 1997.

Siegel, Lee. *Against the Machine: Being Human in the Age of the Electronic Mob.* New York: Spiegel & Grau, 2008.

Solove, Daniel J. *The Future of Reputation: Gossip, Rumor, and Privacy on the Internet.* New Haven: Yale University Press, 2007.

Sunstein, Cass R. *Republic.com 2.0.* Princeton: Princeton University Press, 2007.

Swift, Jonathan. *Major Works.* Edited by Angus Ross and David Woolley. Oxford: Oxford University Press, 1984.

Tocqueville, Alexis de. *Democracy in America.* New York: Random House, 1954.

Vidal, Gore. *Matters of Fact and of Fiction: Essays 1973–1976.* New York: Vintage, 1978.

Wilson, Edmund. *The Shores of Light: A Literary Chronicle of the Twenties and Thirties.* New York: Farrar, Straus & Giroux, 1952.

Wolfe, Tom. *Radical Chic & Mau-Mauing the Flak Catchers.* New York: Farrar, Straus & Giroux, 1970.

Worman, Nancy. *Abusive Mouths in Classical Athens.* Cambridge: Cambridge University Press, 2008.

Young, Toby. *How to Lose Friends & Alienate People: A Memoir.* New York: Da Capo, 2001.

Acknowledgments

T his book was born during a pan-Pacific dinner in Seattle in March 2007, with political journalist Michael Kinsley, Patty Stonesifer (Mike's wife), Susan Rieger (my wife), and me. Somewhere between the Singing Fish Satay and the Pow Wok Lamb, Mike and I, for some reason, said more or less the same thing—that snark was becoming the characteristic discourse of our time. Susan and Patty agreed. Mike, it turned out, was thinking of writing a long essay on snark for a national magazine; I had been toying with the idea of doing a short book about it. He immediately, and somewhat mysteriously, ceded the turf to me, a gift I received with gratitude and also with chagrin, since no one could have written about snark with greater wit than Michael Kinsley.

I would like to thank my literary agent, Kathy Robbins, and Simon & Schuster's editor in chief, Priscilla Painton, for quickly turning a dinner-table conversation into an actual book project; Priscilla for much editorial help and advice; and the rest of the crew at Simon & Schuster, including publisher David Rosenthal and production editor Jonathan Evans, for rapidly bringing the book to press.

I would also like to acknowledge the friends and colleagues who offered information, advice, warnings, and encouragement:

Acknowledgments

Ann Bartow, Peter Blauner, Jane Booth, Henry Breitrose, Richard Brody, Tina Brown, Daniel Cole, Lauren Collins, Max Denby, Thomas Denby, Blake Eskin, Henry Finder, Ben Greenman, Kenneth Gross, John Lahr, Richard McCoy, Paul Muldoon, Daniel Okrent, George Packer, Richard Panek, Maggie Pouncey, Judith Rascoe, David Ratzan, Stephen Schiff, Cathleen Schine, Leonard Schwarz, James Shapiro, Michael Shapiro, Rebecca Traister, Jeremy Waldron, Dorothy Wickenden, Meg Wolitzer, Nancy Worman, Daniel Zalewski, and Diane Zimmerman. Lila Byock did some Internet research for which I am very grateful.

Susan Rieger endured and advanced the project in dozens of ways and fell into snark no more than two or three times.